GREAT VACATIONS
in
Oregon & Washington

GREAT VACATIONS
in
Oregon & Washington

By KiKi Canniff

Published by Ki² Enterprises
1214 Wallace Rd. NW #165
Salem, OR 97304

TABLE OF CONTENTS

Introduction

Leslie Gulch, Oregon

Cascade Loop, Washington

Steens Mountain, Oregon

Long Beach Peninsula, Washington

Pacific Coast, Oregon

Eastern Washington

Columbia River Gorge, Oregon/Washington

Olympic Peninsula, Washington

Wallowa Mountains, Oregon

Mt. St. Helens & Mt. Rainier, Washington

Index

A LETTER FROM THE AUTHOR

Dear Readers,

Many of you have been having fun with my books since 1981. We've explored covered bridges, ghost towns, old forts, museums, parks, campgrounds and thousands of free attractions together. This book will show you the diversity of the scenery in this corner of the continental United States.

Volcanic eruptions, glaciers, prehistoric floods and erosion have all played a part in creating the Pacific Northwest's unique landscape. Although the raw wilderness once revered by its Native Americans has been forever erased in many locales, a significant number of wild places still exist throughout this two state region.

Choosing the region's best vacation areas wasn't an easy task, because I wanted to make sure this book would be just as useful to long-time residents as it would to visitors and newcomers. Having spent most of my adult life exploring and writing about this little corner of the world, you can bet I've discovered lots of one-of-a-kind places.

Great Vacations in Oregon & Washington outlines ten complete family vacation adventures. It will show you where to go for the best views, hiking, swimming, fishing, exploring and historic attractions. Each vacation is followed up by a selection of accommodations, that includes everything from deluxe resorts, bed & breakfasts and RV camps to free campgrounds, youth hostels and inexpensive motels.

I'm an avid explorer, so for me there's always been nothing quite like waking up surrounded by nature. I find the sounds, smells, and sense of adventure exhilarating. My perfect vacation has always included camping, a trail for exploring, and a very real possibility of seeing wildlife.

Having slept in more than 600 of the Pacific Northwest's 2,000 campgrounds, I've pitched my tent in a variety of settings; everything from quiet forest retreats and barren desert camps, to busy lakeside RV parks infested with concrete. But times change, and I now find myself spending just as much time in bed & breakfasts and quaint inns. This book reflects that change.

The vacations I have included in this book will take you to a variety of scenic places. To insure that everyone will be able to find a place to stay, many of the campgrounds and motels I have listed are large and easily accessible. To allow for everyone's budget, a variety of accommodation levels has been included.

VACATION MAP

The shaded areas on this two-state map represent the ten vacations covered in this book.

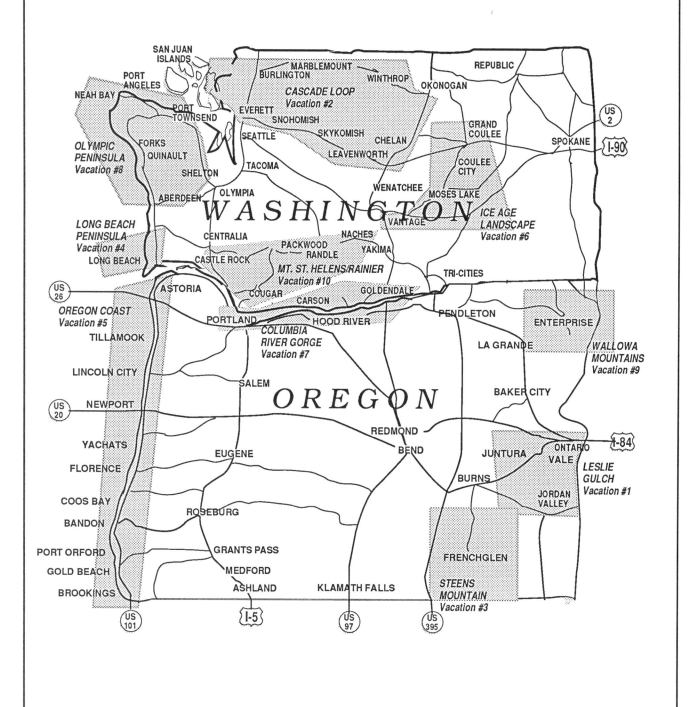

If you have any special interests contact one of the agencies listed at the end of any vacation description for further information. For a complete listing of Oregon and Washington's 2,000 public campgrounds refer to *A Camper's Guide to Oregon & Washington* and *Free Campgrounds of Washington & Oregon.*

A Brief Look at the Vacations

Vacation One - A Stark and Startling Adventure in Leslie Gulch begins near the Oregon/Idaho border, and is the most primitive and unique area included in this book. This remarkable landscape is the result of violent volcanic eruptions followed by 15 million years of natural erosion. The landscape is wondrous, and relatively untouched by mankind. It offers lots of wide-open space and should only be visited by those who intend to keep it pristine.

Vacation Two - Magnificent Journeys along the Cascade Loop gives you a chance to explore northern Washington's Cascade Mountains. It is just as accessible to vacationers driving an RV as those in cars. Whether you intend to cover the entire 400-mile distance or just a short stretch, you'll find plenty of attractions, campgrounds, and inns from which to choose. This vacation will provide you with a close-up look at the lush beauty that has brought people to the Pacific Northwest for hundreds of years.

Vacation Three - High Mountain Trekking on Steens Mountain offers the opportunity to explore Oregon's high desert country. Crystal clear mountain lakes, glacier-carved gorges, wild horses and Oregon's highest road are just a few of the attractions found here. Historic sites, plentiful wildlife, intriguing lava formations, and the famed Great Basin are also an important part of a Steens Mountain vacation.

Vacation Four - Kites, Sunken Ships, Old Forts & the World's Longest Beach are all found along Washington's Long Beach Peninsula. It's really a great place for a family vacation with its wide-open sandy beaches, historic forts, intriguing museums, and a delightful blend of small fishing villages and fun tourist towns.

Vacation Five - Picturesque Encounters at the Oregon Coast points out some of the state's coastal treasures. Nearly all of Oregon's beaches are state-owned, providing public access to 360 miles of beachland. You'll find both white and black sand beaches, agate-strewn coves, rocky waters, and some gorgeous places where the mountains touch the sea. You'll also encounter lots of small towns, friendly people, and great scenery.

Vacation Six - An Ice Age Vacation in Eastern Washington takes you southeast of Coulee Dam, to a desert with a truly unusual background. During the earth's Ice Age, a 600 foot deep wall of water raced across this corner of Washington. It carved deep into the landscape, forever changing it's appearance and carving deep gorges and channels. All this in just two weeks time. Water lovers, as well as those who fish, will also find this vacation's numerous lakes and rivers worth more than one visit.

Vacation Seven - The Best of the Columbia River Gorge will not only show you the national scenic area's better-known waterfalls, public forest land, hiking trails and scenic vistas, but also some great out-of-the way spots. The river provides a chance to watch working tug boats, mammoth grain barges, refurbished sternwheelers, fishing boats, sailboats and other pleasure craft, at work and play. It's also popular with windsurfers.

Vacation Eight - Exploring Washington's Olympic Peninsula will point out moss-draped old-growth forests, spectacular wilderness trails, rugged mountains, relatively untrampled ocean beaches, and the western hemisphere's largest virgin rain forest. Together, the peninsula's Olympic National Park and Olympic National Forest provide public access to a wealth of exceptional places, making it easy for everyone to enjoy this beautiful region.

Vacation Nine - Alpine Adventures in the Wallowa Mountains takes you on a trip to Oregon's northeast corner; a landscape locals refer to as "Little Switzerland." Its mountains include several over 8,000 feet, and offer hundreds of miles of horse and hiking trails. This vacation will take you to see America's deepest river gorge and Wallowa Lake, a 283-foot-deep glacially-carved lake that is filled with giant mackinaw, trout and kokanee.

Vacation Ten - A Two Mountain Odyssey; Mount St. Helens & Rainier provides you with a tour of both the destruction left by Mount St. Helens volcanic eruption, and the serene beauty of Mt. Rainier. Both mountains have paved roadways allowing you to get within a few feet of some pretty spectacular overlooks. Those wanting to really see the area will find hundreds of miles of hiking trails.

So, whether your next Pacific Northwest vacation will be a weekend outing, or a two week trip, I'm sure you'll find a destination or two in this book that will help you to make it unforgettable. I hope you enjoy my favorite places. See you out there!

Happy travels!

KiKi Canniff

Vacation #1

A Stark and Startling
Adventure in Leslie Gulch

The Leslie Gulch Road is a scenic unimproved byway, lined with colorful erosion-carved rock formations. Although mud can make it hard to navigate during rainstorms, most visitors will find that as long as the weather has been fairly dry for the past couple of days, it's an easy drive.

FROM THE AUTHOR'S JOURNAL . . .

I had covered a lot of miles that day, so it was late by the time I got to the Leslie Gulch turnoff. I knew the roads there were unimproved, and was anxious to reach my destination early, in case I was forced to turn back. I had no problem with the roads; what slowed me up was the totally unusual landscape.

Although I'd seen pictures of Leslie Gulch, I found myself completely unprepared, and mesmerized by the stark beauty and rich colors. This is Oregon's most dramatic landscape, and one that is completely different from any other Pacific Northwest setting.

I've always been in awe of the beauty in America's north-west corner, but arriving in Leslie Gulch I felt like a beg-gar at a banquet. The colors changed with the angle of the sun, and when night fell, it was with an all-encom-passing darkness.

Leslie Gulch is not for everyone, for it is without the civi-lized touches that so many expect. I hope that it will always be a pristine, time-sculpted environment whose only visitors are those who respect nature and leave no trace of their stay.

When I left, it was with a deeper respect for mankind's relatively short lifespan in relation to that of the earth.

Notes from my first Leslie Gulch vacation

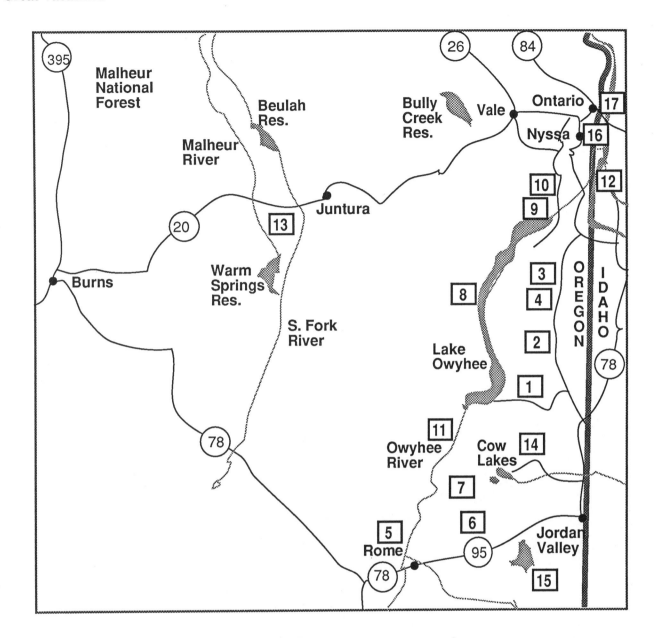

Leslie Gulch Area Attractions

Once you visit Leslie Gulch, it will remain forever in your mind as the Pacific Northwest's most unusual landscape. Located near Oregon's eastern border, it is a place of exceptional beauty. Relatively few people visit this treasure, for it is the rare vacationer who is willing to make the long journey across the state's dry southeastern desert.

Those who cross this arid land will find themselves in a magnificent setting. The gulch is lined with brilliantly colored rock spires that have been sculpted by 15 million years of erosion. Together, the wind, water and time have created a starkly majestic landscape.

Even the region's title is steeped in color. This area was named for a turn-of-the-

Trails are plentiful in Leslie Gulch, making it a great place for hiking or horseback riding.

century cattleman, Hiram Leslie, who was struck by lightening in this gulch in 1882. According to local legend, Leslie had been accused of cattle rustling and, in defending himself, invoked the Lord to strike him dead if he was lying about his innocence. Later that day a lightening bolt knocked him from his horse, and after lingering for a few days, he died.

Colorful Leslie Gulch

Leslie Gulch [1] can be reached from either Jordan Valley or Ontario. From Jordan Valley, take Highway 95 north 18

A variety of birds and small critters build their nests in the gulch's pocked rock walls.

miles to where you will see a sign pointing west toward Leslie Gulch Road. This is the southern route, and will take you through steep-walled canyons, past towering rock spires, columns and pinnacles.

The best time of day to tour the gulch is early morning. When the first rays of sun make their way over the rocks, the range of colors and textures are astounding. Morning is also when you're most likely to see bighorn sheep, antelope, deer, coyotes, wild horses, and lots of birds.

Sundown brings exotic colors to the sandstone and volcanic rock formations, and an eerie stillness to the surroundings. When night falls, it brings total darkness, making it a great place for star gazing.

The Leslie Gulch region has been designated an area of critical environmental concern because of its unique vegetation, outstanding scenery and wildlife. Three wilderness areas, Upper Leslie Gulch, Honeycombs and Slocum Creek, have been established to protect the rare plant species.

There are no lodgings, and only a few campsites within Leslie Gulch. All are primitive. However, there is a variety of parks and accommodations in and near the towns of Ontario, Vale and Nyssa.

Leslie Gulch-Succor Creek Byway [2]
If you're coming from Ontario, you'll find the northern Leslie Gulch entrance near Succor Creek State Park, 40 miles south of town. This road is part of the BLM's National Back Country Byway System. Known as the Leslie Gulch-Succor Creek Byway, this 53-mile route is made up of gravel and dirt roads, with elevations ranging from 2,500 to 4,800 feet.

Succor Creek Canyon [3] is where the region's oldest rock formations can be found. It's also a great place to hunt for picture rock, petrified wood and thundereggs. The creek was at one time an important watering hole for early pioneers. It winds through an impressive rock canyon. You'll find primitive campsites at **Succor Creek State Park [4]** as well as restrooms, picnic facilities and hiking trails.

The byway is not suitable for travel when snowy or wet, and portions are best traveled in a high-clearance vehicle. However, much of the route is accessible to passenger cars as long as you drive carefully. The best time of year to travel the byway is May to October. The road is not recommended for RVs and trailers.

There is no drinking water available along the Leslie Gulch-Succor Creek Byway, so be sure you take plenty of water with you. Before traveling the byway it is also wise to contact the BLM office in Vale for current road conditions.

The Pillars of Rome [5]
Be sure to allow enough time during your vacation in the Leslie Gulch area to see some of the region's other outstanding attractions. No one should miss the Pillars of Rome, or the wild and scenic Owyhee River.

You'll find the Pillars of Rome north of Highway 95; about 20 miles southwest of the town of Jordan Valley. Along the way, you can take a short side trip to view an extinct volcano crater, as well as the grave of Sacajawea's son, John Baptist Charbonneau.

Some of the Pillars of Rome look like ancient Egyptian monuments, others resemble castles. This erosion carved landscape is like no other landscape in the Pacific Northwest.

The Pillars of Rome are an intriguing collection of erosion-carved rocks that have taken on the images of castles and mountain fortresses. Although this, too, is an eroded landscape, it is not at all like of Leslie Gulch.

The rock carvings tower high above a flat desert, like deserted ships on a calm sea. These delicately colored natural rock structures are on private property, so please stay on the road, and enjoy this splendor only from your car.

History buffs will want to take the three-mile drive to **John Baptist Charbonneau's Grave [6]**. Charbonneau was born to Sacajawea as she guided the Lewis and Clark Expedition westward. The turnoff is marked by a small sign, 12 miles west of Jordon Valley. Besides the gravesite, this area holds the rock ruins of Fortified House, Ruby Ranch, and a small ghost town.

Near milepost 12, on Highway 95, you'll see a gravel road leading north. This will take you through the sagebrush-dotted desert to an extinct volcano known as both **Jordan and Coffee Pot Crater [7]**. It's not visible from the highway, and is about a 20-mile drive. The volcano erupted 3,000 to 4,000 years ago and includes a number of smaller spatter cones. The lava flow covers a 30-mile area.

The surrounding landscape is riddled with lava tunnels. Visitors need to exercise extreme caution; it's easy to get hurt on the abrasive lava. Some of those hollow tubes are quite deep, so be careful or you could accidentally fall in, and it's hard to get out alone. There are no facilities at Jordan Crater.

Where to Cool Off

While in the Ontario area, you may wish to allow time to explore Succor Creek itself, swim in beautiful Lake Owyhee, go fishing, soak in a hot spring, or hunt for thundereggs. If you time your visit right, you can also attend the annual Obon Festival or Thunderegg Days.

Owyhee Lake [8] is Oregon's longest lake. Massive rock formations surround the water, creating a haven for trophy size bass. There are also plenty of campsites here, with both a state park and seasonal resort.

The dam, located at the northeast end of the reservoir, is 417 feet high. It's quite spectacular during spring run-off when the overflow cascades wildly into **Glory Hole [9]**. **Snively Hot Springs [10]**, along the Owyhee State Park Road, is also a pleasant treat.

Oregon's **Owyhee River [11]** cuts through a deep, steep-walled canyon that is filled with archeological sites. Some date back 12,000 years.

Floating the Owyhee is the best way to explore this area, but because many parts of the river have rock falls and wild water, it is not for novices. Rapids range from Class I to Class VI.

The river's 120 miles between Owyhee Reservoir and the Oregon/Idaho border are part of the National Wild and Scenic Rivers system. For a detailed boating guide to this area contact the BLM's Vale office.

Where to Fish

Anglers will find several lakes, as well as the Owyhee, **Snake [12]** and **Malheur**

Hikers, especially those with interests in geology or rockhounding, will find plenty of places to explore within Leslie Gulch's three wilderness areas, state park, and BLM acreage.

Rivers [13], worth a visit. Owyhee Lake offers three concrete boat ramps and is stocked with crappie, bass and catfish. **Cow Lakes [14]**, northwest of Jordan Valley, also has a concrete boat ramp. It too is a good place to fish for crappie and bass.

Antelope Reservoir [15], southwest of Jordan Valley, has a gravel boat ramp and a good supply of trout. Catfish weighing over 30 pounds have been caught in the Snake River near Ontario. The Snake also has good crappie, bass and trout fishing.

Rockhounding and Annual Events

Rockhounding is a popular activity around here. The Succor Creek area has thundereggs, Leslie Gulch Canyon moss agates and jasper, and Jordan Valley agates and petrified wood. You can also find obsidian, leaf prints, plume agate, and picture rock.

Every year, beginning on the second Wednesday in July, Nyssa hosts a five-day-long **Thunderegg Days [16]**. This is a good family festival with lots of special activities. One of the most popular activities are the organized tours to local digs where you can learn the art of rock-hounding.

During Thunderegg Days you can tour an extensive rock collection, compliments of the Treasure Valley Rock and Gem Club. You can also purchase thundereggs, garnets, opals, fire agates, picture jasper, petrified wood and other rocks, as well as rockhounding tools and equipment.

Another charming local event is Ontario's annual **Obon Festival [17]**. Generally held the third Saturday in July, it has been observed here for nearly 50 years.

Obon is a Buddhist observance that includes singing, dancing, and traditional Japanese food. In Ontario, it's also a time when Buddhists and non-Buddhists join together for odori dancing to the rhythm of enormous taiko drums. The celebration is based on the legend of Moggallana, a high disciple of Buddha.

Treasure Valley Buddhists have expanded this observance into a celebration of the Japanese culture. Tours of the temple, a variety of Japanese and American foods, authentic Japanese dancing, and other entertainment are included. This festival offers an excellent opportunity to learn about another culture and its traditions.

Whether your idea of a great vacation includes the pulsating drums of the Obon Festival or you're just looking for the quiet solitude of Leslie Gulch Canyon, this area will provide you with an unforgettable experience.

For Additional Information

Call the following agencies as soon as you decide to visit the Leslie Gulch area. Tell them what your interests are and when you are coming. They can provide detailed maps and information that will help you to make your vacation even greater.

Ontario Visitors' Center & Convention Bureau
(888) 889-8012
(541) 889-8012

Nyssa Chamber of Commerce
(541) 372-3091

Vale Chamber of Commerce
(541) 473-3800

Obon Festival
(541) 889-8691

BLM – Vale Office
(541) 473-3144

Oregon State Parks
(800) 452-5687
(If calling from Portland 731-3411)

Leslie Gulch Area Accommodations

NYSSA

Arrowhead Motel (541) 372-3942
710 Emison Ave.
8 rooms, some have microwave & ref.,
pets okay, $40 ($30).

ONTARIO

Best Western Inn (800) 828-0364
251 Goodfellow St. (541) 889-2600
61 units, some w/jacuzzi, pets okay,
handicap access, pool, $46-125.

Budget Colonial Inn (800) 727-5014
1395 Tapadera Ave. (541) 889-9615
84 units, small pets okay, handicap
access, pool, $32-45.

Budget Inn (800) 905-0024
1737 N Oregon St. (541) 889-3101
26 units, 2 w/kitchens, pets okay,
handicap access, pool, $35-75.

Carlile Motel (800) 640-8658
589 N. Oregon (541) 889-8658
18 units - some w/kitchens, small
pets - $5 fee, $36-65.

Holiday Inn (800) 525-5333
1249 Tapadera Ave. (541) 889-8621
98 units, pets okay - $5/night, handi-
cap access, pool, rest./lounge, $69.

Holiday Motor Inn (541) 889-9188
615 E Idaho Ave.
72 units, pets okay, handicap access,
outdoor pool, restaurant, $31-50.

Motel 6 (800) 466-8356
275 NE 12th St. (541) 889-6617
126 units, pets okay, handicap access,
outdoor pool, $28-40.

Oregon Trail Motel (541) 889-8633
92 E Idaho Ave.
30 units, 5 w/kitchens, pets okay,
$25-40.

Plaza Motel (541) 889-9641
1144 SW 4th Ave.
25 units, kitchens, pets okay, $25-35.

Sleep Inn (800) 753-3746
1221 SE First Court (541) 881-0007
65 units, no pets, handicap access,
indoor pool, $40-80.

Stockman's Motel (541) 889-4446
81 SW First St.
28 units, pets okay, handicap access,
nearby restaurant, $28-45.

Super 8 Motel (800) 800-8000
2666 Goodfellow St. (541) 889-8282
63 units, pets okay, handicap access,
indoor pool & jacuzzi, nearby restaurant, $47-53.

VALE

Gold Wheel Motel (541) 473-3947
Junction of Highways 20 & 26
14 units - some w/microwave & ref.,
pets okay, handicap access, walk to
restaurants, $20-30.

Lake Owyhee Resort (541) 339-2444
Lake Owyhee State Park Rd. - 30 miles
south of Vale. (Also accessible from
Ontario & Nyssa.)
11 units plus 7 cabins, all have some
cooking facilities, pets okay, handicap
access, game room, on lake - swimming, fishing, boat launch & docks,
boat rental, tackle shop & groceries,
$45-66.

Leslie Gulch Area Campgrounds & RV Parks

A) Twin Springs BLM Campground

4 units – currently no overnight fee, potable drinking water, vault toilet, primitive, not recommended for trailers - rough road.

Take US Highway 20 west of Ontario 3.5 miles and turn south onto Dry Creek Road. After 2 miles the road will become gravel. Stay to the left and follow it 24.5 miles to the campground.

B) Prospector RV Park

34 campsites – most w/full hookups – $18.00/night, tent area – $5.00/person, showers, laundry, ice, trailer waste disposal. Call (541) 473-3879 for reservation information.

Located in Vale. Take US Highway 26 north of its junction with US Highway 20, and after 3 blocks turn onto Hope Street. The park is 1 block east.

C) Bully Creek Reservoir

66 campsites – most have electricity, showers, trailer waste disposal, swimming, fishing, boat launch, $6.00 to 8.00/night – $36.00 to $50.00/week. For reservations call (541) 473-2969.

Located 9 miles west of Vale via Graham Blvd.

D) Idle Wheels Trailer Park

6 campsites w/full hookups – $15.00/night, no tents, showers, laundry, trailer waste disposal. For reservations call (541) 889-8433.

Located in Ontario, at 198 SE 5th Street.

D) Malheur County Fairgrounds

Open area camping - 20 sites w/elec., tents okay, $5/night, open April thru Oct., restrooms w/flush toilets, trailer waste disposal, information (541) 889-3431.

Located in Ontario, at 795 NW 9th Street.

E) Country Campgrounds

15 campsites w/full hookups – $10.00/night, plus some tent sites – $7.00/night, showers, laundry, trailer waste disposal, picnic area, hiking, fishing. Call (541) 889-6042 for reservation information.

Located 2 miles west of the Ontario airport, at 660 Sugar Avenue.

F) Westerner RV Park

15 campsites w/full hookups – $10.00/night, some sites include cable tv hookups, tents okay, pets okay, showers, laundry, trailer waste disposal, on river, For reservations call (541) 473-3947.

Located in Vale, at the junction of US Highways 20 and 26.

G) Simpson's RV Park

30 pull-thru campsites - 20 w/full hookups plus 10 w/water & electricity, tents okay, $10.00 to $12.00/night - $72.00/week or $195.00/month, restrooms, trailer waste disposal, open year round.

Located in Nyssa, at 498 Columbia Ave.

G) Snively Hot Springs BLM Camp

Primitive campsite clearing – no fee, no drinking water, 136° hot spring.

From Nyssa, take State Highway 201 south 3 miles and turn onto the road to Owyhee State Park. This primitive campground is 1 mile south of the Lower Owyhee Watchable Wildlife Site, about 12 miles north of the reservoir.

H) Lake Owyhee Resort

61 campsites w/water & electricity – $10.00/night, trailers to 35', tents okay, lake, swimming, fishing, boat launch & docks, boat rental, tackle shop & groceries. For reservations call (541) 339-2444.

Head south out of Vale on the road to Lake Owyhee State Park for approximately 38 miles. Also accessible from Ontario & Nyssa.

I) Lake Owyhee State Park

40 sites – 10 w/electricity – $13.00 to $15.00/night, trailers to 55', picnic area, showers, trailer waste disposal, boat launch, fishing, open March-Nov., reservations (800) 551-6949.

Located about 33 miles southwest of Nyssa. Follow the signs to Lake Owyhee State Park.

J) Succor Creek State Park

19 primitive sites – $9.00/night, no drinking water, hiking, picnic area, wildlife viewing site, rockhounding.

Located 30 miles south of Nyssa. Simply follow State Highway 201 to the Succor Creek State Recreation Area Road; the campground is 16.5 miles from this point.

K) Slocum Creek BLM Campground

Primitive camping – no fee, no drinking water, picnic tables, boating, swimming, boat ramp, in Leslie Gulch, on Owyhee River.

Take US Highway 95 north of Jordan Valley 18 miles and go left at the Leslie Gulch turnoff. After about 10 miles you'll reach Leslie Gulch Road; follow it 15 miles to the campground.

L) Rome BLM Campground

6 primitive units – no fee, drinking water, river, boat ramp.

Located at Rome, next to the Owyhee River.

M) Chukar BLM Park

18 units, trailers okay, no hookups, drinking water, on Beulah Reservoir, hiking, $4.00/night.

From Juntura, head west on US Highway 20 to Beulah Reservoir Road then north 6 miles to campground.

N) Idlewild FS Campground

24 units, trailers to 32', no hookups, drinking water, picnic area, in Malheur NF, no fee.

Located on US Highway 395, 17 miles north of Burns.

Vacation #2

Magnificent Journeys
Along the Cascade Loop

Photo courtesy of the Cascade Loop Association

Many beautiful bodies of water lie along the Cascade Loop. Lake Diablo, shown here, is located along the northern half of the loop, and offers great fishing.

FROM THE AUTHOR'S JOURNAL . . .

Every time I tour the Cascade Loop, I am amazed at how close it comes to that picture-perfect image non-residents speak of when fantasizing about a Pacific Northwest vacation.

Towering snow-capped mountains, lush-green forests, wildly rushing rivers, pristine lakes, wildflower-filled mountain meadows and unbelievably gorgeous natural areas are all found along the loop. Looking closely, I catch glimpses of the natural grandeur once seen throughout the Pacific Northwest. I can't help but think to myself, see it now, before all of the old growth trees are gone, for even the young forests are being leveled at a stomach-wrenching rate.

Each Cascade Loop town seems to have its own character, a quiet blend of the cultures that settled the region, and the industries that fueled it. It's a pity so many people speed through these towns without sampling their specialties.

I will have to come back again soon, for this time my visit was much to brief. I must return to Leavenworth in the fall during one of their colorful Bavarian festivals, spend more time hiking along the western shores of Lake Chelan and in the mountains of the North Cascades National Park, and I really should rent a boat again and visit more of the smaller San Juan Islands.

Notes from a tour of the Cascade Loop

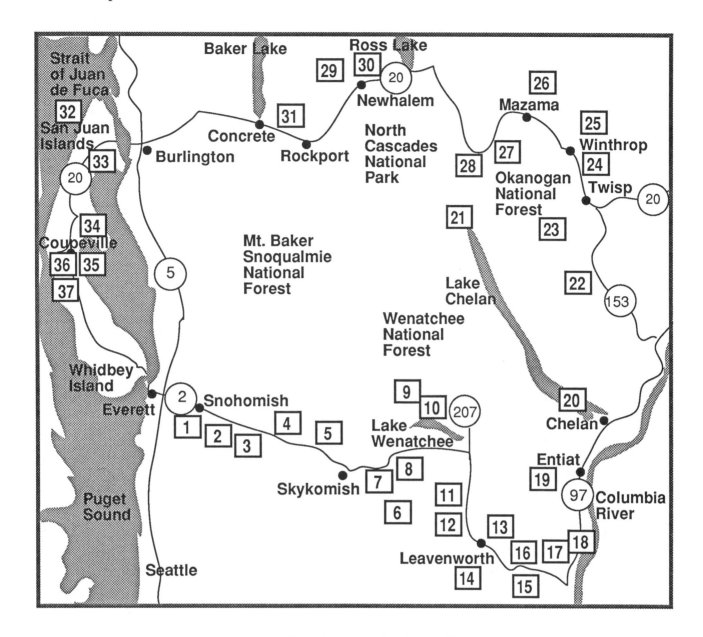

Cascade Loop Attractions

When you drive Washington's Cascade Loop, you follow one of the most spectacular circular routes in America.

This 400-mile drive will take you through vast forests, beside sparkling rivers, into the shadow of snow-capped mountains, past crystal-clear blue-green lakes, into a number of intriguing small towns, and right by lots of great places to spend the night.

There's so much to see along the loop, that you could split the drive into two vacations and still miss spectacular sights. This route crosses the Cascade Mountains twice, meanders alongside several wild and scenic rivers, takes you into three national forests, and to one of America's most scenic national parks.

Getting on the Cascade Loop

The journey begins near Everett; take US Highway 2 east of I-5. A stop in **Snohomish [1]** will give you a chance to shop in the region's greatest collection of antique stores. There are nearly 100 within a four-block area. This turn-of-the-century town has a vintage red-brick downtown area, several historic churches, and lots of elegant old wooden-frame houses.

Traveling east, you'll see the **Skykomish River [2]** along the highway's south side. This river is popular with canoeists, kayakers, and trout fishermen/women.

The state **salmon hatchery [3]** at Startup is a great place to learn about northwest fish. Visitors can walk among the man-made ponds and see salmon ranging in size from tiny fingerlings to mature adults.

Wallace Falls State Park [4], 2 miles northeast of Gold Bar, is the site of a thunderous 250' waterfall. If you follow the 2.5-mile trail to the falls you'll find a panoramic view of the luscious Skykomish Valley.

Continuing on US Highway 2, you soon enter the **Mt. Baker-Snoqualmie National Forest [5]**. The Cascade Mountains have been here for over 15 million years, but this magnificent alpine landscape was created by glaciers within the last 500,000 years.

The Mt. Baker-Snoqualmie National Forest has an office in Skykomish where you can get maps and information. A stop there will enhance your enjoyment of the forest's 1.7 million acres. They can help you find wild rivers, hidden waterfalls, high mountain lakes, year-round glaciers, luscious alpine meadows, and 1400 miles of trails. Backpackers will want to ask about the **Alpine Lakes Wilderness Area [6]**.

Exploring the Stevens Pass Area

As the highway climbs Stevens Pass, you'll see the ferns, mosses and deep woods that typify a mountain rain forest. A good place for a close-up look is **Deception Falls [7]**, just east of Skykomish. A short trail there will lead you through the woods to where the waterfall cascades down the mountainside.

The view from 4,601-foot **Stevens Pass [8]** is expansive. Lofty Mount Index can be seen from one side, the beautiful Skykomish River from the other. The original forest is now gone, but the 6-foot diameter stumps found among the younger trees show the enormous difference between new and old-growth trees.

Stevens Pass has lots of hiking trails. You'll find them along both sides of the road, marked by turnouts and signs. At the summit you can see North America's longest railroad tunnel. It is 7 miles long.

Just beyond Stevens Pass you enter the **Wenatchee National Forest [9]**. Extending 135 miles along the eastern side of the Cascade Mountains, it includes 2.2 million acres and some outstanding recreational lakes. The forest provides 2600 miles of trails through high alpine country and sagebrush-dotted lowlands. The district offices at Lake Wenatchee and Leavenworth are excellent places to get assistance in finding the right trails for your level of endurance.

The **Lake Wenatchee [10]** turnoff is 20 miles east of Stevens Pass. This pristine 7-mile-long lake offers boat launches, swimming beaches, picnic areas, hiking trails, and campgrounds.

Continuing southeast on US Highway 2, you'll soon spot the **Wenatchee River [11]**. It has lots of rapids, waterfalls, and is surrounded by a rugged landscape. The highway has lots of overlooks and trails, which provide easy access to this spectacular terrain.

As the river flows through **Tumwater Canyon [12]**, just west of Leavenworth, the water turns wild. This is a beautiful spot year round, but it's particularly gorgeous in the fall, when the trees change colors.

Delightful Bavarian Shops and Authentic Log Cabins

Downtown **Leavenworth [13]** has been recreated to resemble a Bavarian-style village. It is filled with old-world-style architecture, lots of flowers, specialty shops and German restaurants.

Leavenworth is surrounded by mountains, and resembles a Bavarian village. The citizens put on a number of ethnic activities and celebrations. Contact the Leavenworth Chamber of Commerce for a complete list of these events.

If you follow **Icicle River Road [14]** out of Leavenworth, you can watch rock climbers scale the steep mountains. They come from all over the world to test their skills on these sheer granite cliffs. If you have a good pair of binoculars you can follow individual climbers all the way to the top.

Continuing on US Highway 2, stop in Cashmere for a tour of the **Aplets & Cotlets candy kitchen [15]**. Tours are given June to December, on weekdays between 8:00 a.m. and 5:00 p.m., except during the noon hour, and 10:00 a.m. to 4:00 p.m. most weekends.

Cashmere also has one of the nation's finest collections of pioneer log cabins. Located at the east end of the Cottage Avenue Bridge, the **Chelan County Museum [16]** is open April to October. Hours are 10:00 a.m. to 4:30 p.m. Monday thru Saturday, and 12:30 p.m. to 4:30 p.m. on Sundays.

The cabins have been furnished to depict frontier life in the 1800s. Buildings include a one-room school, post office, barber shop, general store, assay office, millinery shop, jail, doctor's office, saloon, blacksmith shop, mission, railroad depot, print shop, and homestead cabins.

US Highway 97 to Lake Chelan

Just past Cashmere the Cascade Loop takes you north on US Highway 97. This is where you'll find the magnificent **Ohme Gardens [17]**. The work of one family, the gardens took several decades to create and offer a terrific view of the Wenatchee and Columbia River Valleys. The gardens are open daily, April to October, from 9:00 a.m. to dusk. The charge is $5.00 for adults, and $3.00 for children aged 7 thru 17.

At **Rocky Reach Dam [18]**, just north of here, you can take a free tour that begins with a hands-on exhibit explaining hydro-electricity. Other displays cover the Columbia River from prehistoric times to the present, early Indian life, and the huge paddlewheel boats that traveled these rivers in the late 1800s.

Continuing north on US Highway 97, anglers may want to take a side-trip up the **Entiat River [19]**. The fishing is good, and there are several campgrounds.

The next loop highlight is spectacular **Lake Chelan [20]**. If you don't take the boat tour, you'll miss out on a rare treat. This gorgeous 55-mile-long lake ends in the **Lake Chelan National Recreation Area [21]**.

Crystal-clear Lake Chelan sits in a glacier trough that measures over 8,500 feet from valley crest to lake bottom. Much of the surrounding land is accessible only by boat. You'll find a wealth of hiking trails leading to high mountain lakes, year round glaciers, panoramic vistas, hidden waterfalls and pools.

Two passenger ferries operate between the town of Chelan and the head of the lake. The *Lady of the Lake* runs daily, May thru October. Departing at 8:30 a.m., it stops in Stehekin for 1.5 hours, getting back to Chelan by 6:00 p.m. The cost is $22.00 round trip, $11.00 for children 6 to 11, and kids under 6 are free.

Photo courtesy of the Cascade Loop Association

Lake Chelan is one of Washington's most beautiful lakes. It sits surrounded by gorgeous scenery, high in the foothills of the Cascade Mountains. The best way to see it is to take the passenger ferry to Stehekin and spend some time hiking in the woods.

The *Lady Express* makes a faster journey. It leaves at 8:30 a.m., but is back at Chelan by 2:30 p.m. and only stops for an hour in Stehekin. Their new catamaran promises an even speedier journey, departing at 7:45 a.m. and 1:30 p.m. and returning four hours later.

The cost is $41.00, and kids 2 through 10 go for half price. Prepaid reservations are available on the *Lady Express*, call (509) 682-4584. You don't have to return the same day, and can go up the lake on one boat and return on the other.

Methow Valley and an Old West Town

Continuing on the Cascade Loop, you take State Highway 153 into the **Methow Valley [22]**. You'll find this road about 20 miles north of Chelan. It's a peaceful route that follows the Methow River through a wide basin.

The **Okanogan National Forest [23]** is west of the river. This is one of America's oldest national forests; most of its 1.5 million acres were set aside in 1897. The forest provides lots of hiking trails and camp sites. Stop at the ranger station in Twisp for personalized help in deciding where to go.

Heading northwest on State Highway 20, you'll soon arrive in **Winthrop [24]**. This quaint little town recaptures the spirit of the old west. Its main street is lined with false-front buildings, wooden sidewalks, old-fashioned street lights, hitching posts, and watering troughs. Winthrop has the look of an 1890's mining town. You expect a stage to race through town at any moment.

A visit to Winthrop's 1897 **Waring Castle [25]** will teach you a lot about life here prior to the 20th century. This little museum is packed with pioneer memorabilia, Indian artifacts, antique printing equipment, horse-drawn vehicles, and even a few early automobiles. Situated on a hill behind town, the grounds provide a lovely view of the surrounding area. The museum is open daily from 9:00 a.m. to 8:00 p.m. during the sum-

mer. The balance of the year it is open weekends only, from 10:00 a.m. to 5:00 p.m.

Mountain Pass Overlooks

Heading west along State Highway 20, you begin the drive back over the Cascade Mountains. The scenery is gorgeous, yet looks quite different from the southern portion of this loop drive. Dozens of scenic overlooks and hiking trails can be visited along the way.

Washington, Harts and Rainy Pass are three especially scenic viewpoints. The road to **Harts Pass [26]** is 12 miles west of Winthrop, near the Early Winters Forest Service Information Center.

Winthrop will make you feel like you've stepped back in time. The citizens have refurbished it to look like an old-west town.

Follow it 20 miles northwest for a spectacular view. This road is not recommended for trailers.

West of Mazama, about 16 miles, is where you'll find the **Washington Pass Overlook [27]**. It's only .5 mile off the highway. At the end of this paved road you'll find plenty of parking, and a wheelchair-accessible trail.

The view looks out over Early Winters Creek, and is dominated by Liberty Bell Mountain. This 5,477-foot-high overlook is surrounded by massive granite cliffs and snow capped mountains.

Rainy Pass [28] is just west of the Washington Pass overlook road, and where the Pacific Crest Trail crosses the highway. This 2,600-mile trail follows the Cascade Mountain Range from Canada to Mexico. Take the 1-mile paved overlook trail for a great view of the mountains and valleys around Rainy Pass.

North Cascades National Park

Leaving Rainy Pass, the highway takes you downhill 30 miles to Ross Lake. This portion of your drive leads you through parts of the Okanogan National Forest and into the **Ross Lake National Recreation Area [29]**. The grandeur and beauty of this mountainous region is unforgettable.

Your travels will take you right past **Ross, Diablo and Gorge Lakes [30]**. All three are beautiful. You'll see the luscious blue-green waters of Ross and Diablo to the north, as you start down the hill. There are plenty of scenic overlooks where you can safely pull out of traffic to enjoy the view.

Between June 1st and Labor Day you can take a 4-hour excursion that includes a boat cruise on Lake Diablo, a tour of the Ross Dam powerhouse, and a ride up Sourdough Mountain on one of America's last incline railways. Reservations are required. Call Seattle City Light at (206) 684-3030 for details.

In 1968, North Cascades National Park was created to protect this region's wild alpine environment from further development. The 700,000-acre park has beautiful glaciated canyons, towering granite peaks, crystal clear lakes and year-round glaciers.

The park lands have very few roads, but lots of hiking trails. A number of trailheads are found along the North Cascades Highway, as well as Cascade River Road southeast of Marblemount.

If you intend to camp in the back-country, stop at any of the park's ranger stations for directions and a permit. There's no cost for this permit, but it helps the rangers to disperse visitors to avoid overuse. The visitors' center at Newhalem is another good place to get hiking information and permits.

You'll find the 1500-acre **Skagit River Bald Eagle Sanctuary [31]** between Marblemount and Concrete. There are several highway turn-outs near the primary viewing areas, making it easy to safely watch this symbolic American bird. If you look in the tops of the trees along the river, you'll have a good chance

Photo courtesy of the Cascade Loop Association

North Cascades National Park is perhaps one of America's least-celebrated national parks. With its lush forests and sparkling lakes, it's a regional treasure you won't want to miss.

of seeing some of these magnificent birds.

The San Juan Islands

Continuing west on State Highway 20, you are nearing the end of the Cascade Loop, and the beautiful **San Juan Islands [32]**. You can drive right onto two of the islands, Fidalgo and Whidbey. A bridge over Cornet Bay, at Deception Pass, connects the two.

From **Deception Pass State Park [33]** you have a spectacular view that includes several of the smaller islands within the San Juan Archipelago. Some of these are wildlife refuges and parks, but you need a boat to reach them. Camping and water sports, including scuba diving, are popular at the Deception Pass park.

Whidbey Island provides a pastoral setting and is where you'll find several important historic sites. The town of **Coupeville [34]** is filled with authentic false-front buildings. You'll also find an 1855 blockhouse, 1852 log cabin, some turn-of-the-century churches and lots of houses built between 1854 and 1899. The entire town is listed on the National Register of Historic Places.

At the **Island County Historical Museum [35]**, in Coupeville, you can learn about the area's history and pick up a self-guided tour map. The map will show you where you'll find Whidbey Island's most important historic sites, including the **Ebey's Landing National Historic Reserve [36]** and old Fort Casey.

Fort Casey [37] was built in the late 1890s, and is now a state park. Facilities include an informative inter-pretive center, a few campsites and an underwater reserve.

To complete the Cascade Loop, take the ferry on the southeast tip of Whidbey Island to the mainland town of Everett. It's a short trip, and the ferry runs every 30 minutes. The view from the water is beautiful, and in late spring and early winter you can hear sea lions barking.

The ferry ride will cost $7.50 for two adults and a passenger car. Seniors, and those on bicycles or motorcycles, pay less and vehicles longer than 20' or taller than 7'6" cost more.

For Additional Information

If you plan on visiting this area, call the Cascade Loop Association and ask for their free color booklet. It's packed with photos, maps and all kinds of helpful information. Hikers might also call the national forest or park they intend to explore.

Cascade Loop Association
(509) 662-3888

North Cascades N. Park & Mt. Baker-Snoqualmie N. Forest
(360) 856-5700

Wenatchee National Forest
(509) 662-4335

Okanogan National Forest
(509) 826-3275

Washington State Parks
(800) 233-0321

Washington State Ferries
(206) 464-6400

Cascade Loop Area Accommodations
(Towns listed in same order as Cascade Loop Vacation.)

SNOHOMISH

Inn at Snohomish (800) 548-9993
323 Second St. (360) 568-2208
21 rooms w/private baths - some
w/jacuzzi, no pets, includes pass to
public pool, walk to restaurants &
antique row, $69-95 ($65-85).

Nita's on Ninth St. (360) 568-7081
425 Ninth St.
3 rooms - 2 w/private bath in 1884
Queen Anne Victorian home, inc. full
breakfast, seasonal pool, no smoking,
no pets, older children okay, near
antique row & shops, $85-95.

Redmond House B&B (360) 568-2042
317 Glen Ave.
4 suites - 2 w/private bath in 1890
historic home, inc. formal breakfast,
hot tub in solarium, game room,
veranda & gardens, no pets, kids okay,
walk to antique row, $85-100.

Snohomish Grand Valley Inn
11910 Springetti Rd. (360) 568-8854
5 rooms - 3 in rural farmhouse plus 2
in refurbished barn - most have private bath, inc. country breakfast, this
is a working farm, kids welcome, pets
okay, $55-95.

SULTAN

Dutch Cup Motel (800) 844-0488
918 Main (360) 793-2215
21 rooms, small ref., pets okay - $7
fee, walk to rest./lounge, $51-68.

SKYKOMISH

SkyRiver Inn (800) 367-8194
333 River Dr. E. (360) 677-2261
16 rooms plus 2 suites - some have
kitchenette, quiet, on Skykomish
River, pets okay - $2 fee, $61-76.

LEAVENWORTH

Albenblume Pension (800) 669-7634
12570 Ranger Rd. (509) 548-4059
6 rooms w/baths - some w/fireplace &
whirlpool baths, $77-159.

AlpenRose Inn B&B (800) 582-2474
500 Alpine Pl. (509) 548-3000
15 rooms w/private baths - some
w/jaccuzi, outdoor pool & hot tub, no
smoking, no pets or young children,
$75-150.

Best Western Icicle Inn
(800) 558-2438 or (509) 548-7000
505 US Hwy. 2
90 units, jacuzzi suites, year round
pool & spa, exercise room, includes
breakfast buffet, walk to downtown,
located next to fun park, $85-179.

Bindlestiff's Riverside Cabins
1600 US Hwy. 2 (509) 548-5015
8 cabins w/private baths overlooking
whitewater, most inc. ref., pets okay -
$7 fee, $55-65.

Enzian Motor Inn (800) 223-8511
590 US Hwy. 2 (509) 548-5269
104 Austrian-decorated rooms plus 7
suites, some w/jacuzzi & fireplace,
$78-167.

Evergreen Inn (800) 327-7212
1117 Front St. (509)548-5515
rooms & suites - some w/kitchens,
includes European breakfast, pets
okay, outdoor hot tubs, $62-127.

Haus Lorelei (800) 514-8868
347 Division (509) 548-5726
rooms w/private baths in 1903
European-style mansion, inc. gourmet
breakfast & afternoon tea, no smoking, kids okay, on Wenatchee River,
outdoor hot tub, tennis & basketball
court, walk to downtown & restaurants, $89-99 ($75-80).

Haus Rohrbach Pension
(800) 548-4477 or (509) 548-7024
12882 Ranger Rd.
5 suites w/private baths plus 3 rooms
w/private bath & 2 w/shared bath,
inc. European-style breakfast, some
units have microwave, ref., whirlpool
tub and fireplace, pool, year round
spa, no smoking, $75-160 ($75-95).

Hotel Pension Anna (800) 509-ANNA
926 Commercial St. (509) 548-6273
12 rooms + 3 suites - Austrian-style
decor., private baths, suites have fireplace & jacuzzi, $80-175.

Lake Wenatchee Hide-a-Ways
(800) 883-2611 or (509) 548-9074
9762 North Rd.
10 cabins w/kitchens, $100-175,
some have hot tub, some pets okay.

Mountain Home Lodge
(800) 414-2378 or (509) 548-7077
8201-9 Mountain Home Rd.
10 rooms w/private baths, outdoor hot
tub & pool, tennis courts, restaurant,
summer rates inc. breakfast - winter
all meals, no smoking, $100-180
($200-330).

Mountain Springs Lodge
19115 Chiwawa Rd. (800) 858-2276
7 buildings offering everything from 1
room suites to large group accommodations - some w/kitchen/jacuzzi/hot
tub, no pets, no smoking, $125-350.

Mrs. Anderson's Lodging House
(800) 253-8990
917 Commercial St. (509) 548-6173
7 rooms w/bath plus 2 w/shared
bath, non-smoking, furnished
w/antiques & quilts, $47-73.

Obertal Motor Inn (800) 537-9382
922 Commercial St. (509) 548-5204
rooms & suites w/private baths in
Bavarian-style inn, inc. breakfast, outdoor hot tub, handicap access, pets
okay, $63-101.

Pine River Ranch (800) 669-3877
19668 Hwy. 207 (509) 763-3959
rooms & suites - some w/fireplace,
jacuzzi, micro./ref., inc. breakfast, hot
tub, no smoking or pets, $89-150.

Rodeway Inn (800) 693-1225
185 US Hwy. 2 (509) 548-7992
33 rooms - family suites, fireplace &
jacuzzi rooms available, indoor pool,
outdoor hot tub, handicap accessible
rooms, pets okay, $69-119 ($59-119).

Run of the River
(800) 288-6491 or (509) 548-7171
9308 E. Leavenworth Rd.
6 rooms - some w/whirlpool & wood
stove, hot tub, no smoking, $95-150.

Saimon's Hide-a-Ways (800) 845-8638
16408 River Rd. (509) 763-3213
7 cabins w/kit. & hot tub, on Wenatchee River, no smoking, $95-145.

CHELAN

Brick House Inn Bed & Breakfast
(800) 799-2332 or (509) 682-2233
304 Wapato St.
5 rooms in a 1910 Victorian house -
some w/private bath and kitchenette,
no smoking, no pets or kids, $68-87.

Campbell's Resort (800) 553-8225
104 W. Woodin Ave. (509) 682-2561
170 rooms plus 3 cottages - some
w/kitchens, two outdoor pools & hot
tub, on Lake Chelan, rest./lounge,
$138-322 ($60-166).

Captain's Quarters (509) 682-5886
283 Minneapolis Beach Rd.
2 suites w/jacuzzis plus 1 room, all
have private bath & sunroom, includes
bountiful breakfast on deck overlooking Lake Chelan, no smoking or pets,
older kids okay, $115-135 ($75-85).

Caravel Resort (800) 962-8723
322 W. Woodin Ave. (509) 682-2582
92 rooms - some 2 bedroom suites
w/kitchens, on Lake Chelan, outdoor
hot tub & pool, walk to downtown,
$107-308 ($52-132).

Darnell's Resort Motel
(800) 967-8149 or (509) 682-2015
901 Spader Bay Rd.
38 rooms w/kitchenette in older family
motel, pool & hot tub, 9-hole putting
green, tennis court, canoes, bicycles,
walk to restaurants, $159 ($60).

Inn Above The Lake (509) 682-3184
914 Cone Rd.
2 rooms + 2 bedroom suite w/private baths, lake view, no smoking, indoor sauna & hot tub, outdoor pool, older children okay, $115-150 ($75-90).

Midtowner Motel (509) 682-4051
721 E. Woodin Ave.
45 rooms - 6 w/kitchenettes, all inc. ref./micro., hot tub, pool, laundry, walk to downtown, $60-70 (40-45).

Silver Bay Inn (800) 555-7781
10 Silver Bay Rd. (509) 682-2212
B&B plus 2 cabins on Lake Chelan, B&B - private bath & deck, hot tub, private beach, canoes, bikes, no pets, no smoking, older children okay, no credit cards, $85-150.

Stehekin Valley Ranch
(800) 536-0745 or (509) 682-4677
In Stehekin @ head of Lake Chelan
5 cabins w/private bath & tent cabins w/shared bathhouse, open mid-June to Oct., $60-70/person inc. meals.

Whaley Mansion (800) 729-2408
Chelan (509) 682-5735
6 elegant rooms w/baths in Victorian mansion, no kids, pets or smoking, walk to lake, $115+ - inc. breakfast.

Wapato Point Resort
(888) 768-9511 or (509) 687-9511
1 Wapato Way - Manson
1-3 bedroom condos on 116 acres, 7 outdoor pools, lighted tennis courts, mini-golf, rest./lounge, no pets, on Lake Chelan, $155-275 ($75-150).

Wapato Point Village Inn
(800) 771-5300 or (509) 687-2500
200 Wapato Point Ct. - Manson
10 suites w/kitchens, 1 wheelchair unit, rest./lounge, BBQ/picnic area, quiet, walk to lake, no pets, $95 ($59).

Westview Resort Motel
2312 W. Woodin Ave. (509) 682-4396
25 rooms/suites plus 2 cabins, on Lake Chelan, hot tub, pri. beach, outdoor pool, handicap access, $115-165 ($54-115).

WINTHROP

Best Western Cascade Inn
(800) 468-6754 or (509) 996-3100
960 Hwy. 20
63 rooms, pool, hot tub, on Methow River, nearby rest., $80-100 ($50-60).

Chewuch Inn (800) 747-3107
223 White Ave. (509) 996-3107
8 rooms - 2 w/kitchenettes, plus 4 cabins w/kitchenettes, inc. continental plus breakfast, walk to restaurants, $60-85 ($50-65).

Hotel Rio Vista (800) 398-0911
285 Riverside (509) 996-3535
16 rooms overlooking Methow River in western-style downtown hotel, hot tub, no smoking, $85 ($45-65).

River Run Inn (800) 757-2709
27 Rader Rd. (509) 996-2173
11 rooms, some w/kitchenette, plus 2 bedroom cabin & 6 bedroom house, pool & spa, walk to town, rooms $80-85 ($60-70) - cabin $150 ($130) - house $310-350 (285-335).

Sun Mountain Lodge (800) 572-0493
Patterson Lake Rd. (509) 996-2211
115 rooms - 13 inc. kitchenette, 2 pools, 3 hot tubs, rental canoes & horses, activities, on Lake Patterson, $145-250 ($110-190).

Trail's End Motel (509) 996-2303
Downtown Winthrop
12 rooms, sauna, walk to restaurants, $63-68 (call for off-season rates).

Winthrop Inn (800) 444-1972
960 Hwy. 20 (509) 996-2217
30 units w/ref. & microwave, inc. continental breakfast, pool, hot tub, on Methow River, no smoking, pets okay, nearby restaurant, $65-80 ($50-70).

CONCRETE-ROCKPORT

A Cab in the Woods (360) 873-4106
East of Rockport @ MP103 on Hwy. 20
5 cedar log cabins w/kitchens & private baths, quiet & cozy, kids welcome, pets okay, $65-75 ($55-65).

Clark's Cabins, RV & Restaurant
(360) 873-2250
6 miles east of Rockport
3 rooms plus 27 cabins and 6 travel trailers, kitchens, pets okay - $10 fee, $40-109 ($35-69).

North Cascade Inn (800) 251-3054
4284 State Hwy. 20 (360) 853-8870
14 rooms, rest./lounge, no pets, $50.

Ovenell's Heritage Inn B& B
(360) 853-8494
46276 Concrete-Sauk Valley Rd.
6 rooms - 3 w/private bath, on working ranch, no pets, $80-115 ($70-105), includes breakfast.

WHIDBEY ISLAND
COUPEVILLE

Anchorage Inn (360) 678-5581
807 N Main St.
5 rooms w/bath in historic home, inc. break., no kids/pets/smoking, walk to rest., open Feb.-Nov., $75-95.

Captain Whidbey Inn
(800) 366-4097 or (360) 678-4097
2072 W Captain Whidbey Inn Rd.
37 rooms in 1907 inn plus cabins & cottages, on Penn Cove, rest./lounge, no pets, $95-225 ($54-175).

Inn at Penn Cove (360) 678-8000
702 Main St.
6 rooms - 4 w/bath - in two historic homes, inc. break., no smoking/pets, $60-125.

The Victorian B&B (360) 678-5305
602 Main St.
2 rooms w/bath in historic Victorian home plus guest cottage, inc. breakfast, $80-100.

Tyee Restaurant & Motel
405 S Main St. (360) 678-6616
9 rooms, handicap access, restaurant, pets okay - $10 fee, downtown, $46 ($39).

WHIDBEY ISLAND
OAK HARBOR

A Country Pillow (360) 675-4608
119 E Troxell Rd.
2 cottages, inc. cont. breakfast, beach access, no pets/kids, $75-95.

Acorn Motor Inn (800) 280-6646
31530 State Hwy. 20 (360) 675-6646
27 units, some w/kitchenettes, inc. cont. breakfast, pets okay, $52-68.

Auld Holland Inn (800) 228-0148
33575 State Hwy. 20 (360) 675-2288
34 rooms, inc. cont. breakfast, jacuzzi suites & kitchen units, pool, spa, gym, rest./lounge, pets okay, $55-85.

Best Western Harbor Plaza
(800) 927-5478 or (360) 679-4567
33175 State Hwy. 20
80 rooms w/ref. & micro., inc. cont. breakfast, pool, spa, exercise room, rest./lounge, pets okay, $79-129.

Coachman Inn (800) 635-0043
32959 State Hwy. 20 (360) 675-0727
102 units, inc. cont. breakfast, jacuzzi suites & kitchen units, exercise room, pool, spa, laundry, no pets, $60-175.

Inn at the Bay B&B (360) 679-8320
5129 N Alto Lane
1 unit w/pri. bath, inc. full breakfast, no pets or smoking, $80.

North Island B&B (360) 675-7080
1589 N West Beach Rd.
2 fireplace units w/private bath, inc. breakfast buffet, no kids, pets or smoking, $90.

North Whidbey Inn (360) 675-5911
461 SE Midway Blvd.
17 units - some w/kitchens, no pets, $45-80.

Victorian Rose B&B (360) 675-8197
438 E Sea Breeze Way
4 rooms w/shared baths in Victorian farmhouse, inc. full breakfast, jacuzzi, no kids/pets/smoking, $75-125.

Cascade Loop Campgrounds & RV Parks

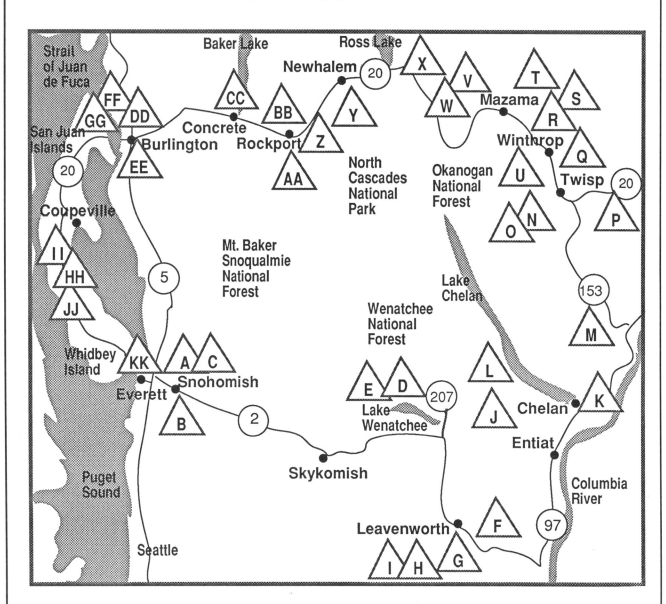

A) FLOWING LAKE COUNTY PARK

28 RV sites w/water & elec., plus 10 tent sites, 3 sites for disabled - can be reserved (360) 568-2274, flush toilets, picnic area, boat launch, swimming, fishing, pets okay, $10 to $14/night.

In Snohomish. Turn left off US Hwy. 2 at milepost #10, drive 5 miles to 48th Avenue and turn right. The park is at the end of the road.

A) SNOHOMISH GR. VLY INN CAMP

3 individual campsites w/elec., plus small group tent area on working farm, shower.

Located about 2 miles south of Snohomish. Follow State Hwy. 9 to Marsh Road and turn right. When you get to the T turn right again onto Springetti Rd. The camp is located at 11910 Springetti Rd.

B) MONEY CREEK FS CAMP

24 sites (14 can be reserved - (800) 280-CAMP), trailers to 22', group sites, pit toilets, picnic area, well water, swimming, fishing, in Mt. Baker-Snoqualmie NF, pets okay, $12/night.

Take US Hwy. 2 west of Skykomish 2.5 miles, and FSR 6400 southeast .1 mile.

C) BECKLER RIVER FS CAMP

27 campsites (18 can be reserved - (800) 280-CAMP), trailers to 22', well water, pit toilets, fire pits w/grills, picnic tables, fishing, swimming, in Mt. Baker-Snoqualmie NF, pets okay, $12/night.

Drive east of Skykomish 1 mile on US Hwy. 2, and take FSR 65 north 2 miles.

D) NASON CREEK FS CAMP

73 campsites, trailers to 32', piped water, flush toilets, on river, fishing, hiking trail, in Wenatchee NF, pets okay, elev. 1800', $10/night.

Located northeast of the US Hwy. 2 & State 207 junction. Take State Hwy. 207 northeast 3.4 miles to CR 290; campground is west .1 mile.

E) LAKE WENATCHEE STATE PARK

197 units, no hookups, res. req. - (800) 452-5687, picnic shelter, wheelchair access, trailer waste disposal, summer programs, boat launch, fishing, swimming, pets okay, $10 to $11/night.

Go north of US Hwy. 2 & State Hwy. 207 junction 6 miles on State 207.

F) TUMWATER FS CAMP

84 units, no hookups, large group site w/shelter - res. req. (800) 274-8104, trailers to 20', picnic area, handicap access, stream, flush toilets, fishing, hiking, in Wenatchee NF, pets okay, elev. 2050', $11/night.

Northwest of Leavenworth 9.9 miles on US Hwy. 2.

G) ICICLE RIVER RANCH

64 campsites, 52 w/full hookups, plus 12 tent sites, reservation information - (509) 548-5420, showers, spa, putting green, river, swimming, fishing, $16 to 25/night.

Leave US Hwy. 2 about .5 mile southwest of town. Campground is 3 miles, at 7305 Icicle Road.

H) PINE VILLAGE KOA

135 campsites - 46 w/full hookups, 60 w/water & elec., plus 29 tent sites, reservations (509)548-7709, showers, laundry, groceries, picnic shelter, playground, trailer waste disposal, swimming pool, hot tub for adults, river, swimming, fishing, hiking, pets okay, open mid-March thru Sept., $23 to $30/night.

Located at 11401 River Bend Dr. - take US Hwy. 2 east .3 mile and follow River Bend Dr. north .5 mile

H) EIGHTMILE FS CAMP

45 units, large group site - reservation required - (509) 548-6977, trailers to 20', handicap access, handicap accessible vault toilets, hand pump well, stream, fishing, hiking, in Wenatchee NF, elev. 1800', $9/night.

Southwest of Leavenworth. Leave US Hwy. 2 .5 mile southwest of town on Icicle Road. Campground is 8 miles.

I) JOHNNY CREEK FS CAMP

65 units, trailers to 20', hand pump well, handicap accessible vault toilets, fishing, hiking, in Wenatchee NF, elev. 2300', $8 to $9/night.

Southwest of Leavenworth. Leave US Hwy. 2 .5 mile southwest of town on Icicle Road. Campground is 12.4 miles.

J) SILVER FALLS FS CAMP

35 units - 4 trailers to 22' plus small group site, reservation required for group site - (509) 784-1511, picnic area, hand pump wells, stream, 150' natural waterfall, fishing, hiking, in Wenatchee NF, pets okay, elev. 2400', $10/night.

Northwest of Entiat. Leave US Hwy. 97 1.4 miles southwest of town on Entiat

River Road. Campground is 30.4 miles northwest.

K) CITY OF CHELAN LAKESHORE WATERFRONT RV PARK

160 units - 151 w/full hookups, plus 9 w/water & elec. – tents okay, no dogs in summer, information - (509) 682-8023, reservations by mail only, showers, playground, trailer waste disposal, on Lake Chelan, swimming, fishing, bumper & paddle boats, go carts, mini golf, no pets or fires, $11 to $26/night.

In Chelan, right on State Hwy. 150.

L) LAKE CHELAN STATE PARK

146 units, 17 w/full hookups, reservations available in summer – (509) 687-3710, wheelchair access, picnic shelter, on Lake Chelan, snack bar, trailer waste disposal, boat launch, scuba diving area, fishing, swimming, water skiing, $10 to $16/night.

Leave Chelan heading west on the road leading around the south side of Lake Chelan. Campground is 9 miles.

M) ALTA LAKE STATE PARK

1981 units, 31 w/water & electricity, community kitchen, wheelchair access, trailer waste disposal, fishing, swimming, trail, $10 to $15/night.

Take US Hwy. 97 northeast of Chelan 17 miles, then State Hwy. 153 west 2 miles to campground road, and follow south 2 miles to park.

N) POPLAR FLAT FS CAMP

16 units, trailers to 22', pit toilets, picnic area, piped water, river, wheelchair access, fishing, hiking, in Okanogan NF, pets okay, $5/night (must buy pass in Twisp or Winthrop), information - (509) 826-3275.

Leave Twisp on CR 9114 and head west 10.8 miles, then take FSR 44 northwest 9.4 miles.

O) BLACK PINE LAKE FS CAMP

23 units, trailers to 22', pit toilets, picnic area, piped water, lake - no motors, wheelchair access, boat launch, boating, fishing, hiking, in Okanogan NF,

pets okay, $5/night (must buy pass in Twisp or Winthrop), information - (509) 826-3275.

Leave Twisp on CR 9114 and head west 11 miles, then take FSR 43 south 8 miles.

P) RIVER BEND RV PARK

104 campsites, 69 w/full hookups, plus 35 tent sites, information - (509) 997-3500, showers, laundry, rec hall, playfield, playground, trailer waste disposal, fishing, $14 to $18/night.

Southeast of Twisp 6 miles on State Hwy. 20.

Q) METHOW RVR/WINTHROP KOA

120 campsites, 16 w/full hookups, 52 w/water & electricity, plus 52 tent units, (509) 996-2258, showers, laundry, groceries, trailer waste disposal, heated swimming pool, river, fishing, playground, $20 to $25/night.

Southeast of Winthrop 1 mile on State Hwy. 20.

R) PEARRYGIN LAKE STATE PARK

84 units, 30 w/full hookups, 27 w/water only, info. (509) 996-2370 - res. (800) 452-5687, wheelchair access, trailer waste disposal, boat launch, fishing, $10 to $16/night.

At Winthrop, take Riverside north .5 mile, Bluff Street east 2 miles, and follow Pearrygin Lake Road to campground.

S) DERRY'S RESORT ON PEARRYGIN LAKE

154 campsites, 64 w/full hookups, plus 90 tent units, reservations - (509) 996-2322, showers, laundry, groceries, playground, trailer waste disposal, on lake, fishing, swimming, boat launch, $15 to $18/night.

Leave Winthrop on Riverside and go north .5 mile to Bluff Street, then east 2 miles to Pearrygin Lake Road. Camp is east 1 mile.

T) FLAT FS CAMP

12 units, trailers to 18', pit toilets, stream, wheelchair access, fishing, in Okanogan NF, no garbage service, pets

okay, $5/night (must buy pass in Twisp or Winthrop), information - (509) 826-3275..

Head north of Winthrop 6.6 miles on CR 1213, 2.8 miles on FSR 51, and northwest 2 miles on FSR 5130 to camp.

U) BIG TWIN LAKE CAMPGROUND

86 units - 20 w/full hookups, 26 w/water & elec., 40 w/out hookups, plus tenting area, res. - (509)996-2650, pull-thrus, showers, laundry, trailer waste disposal, playground, lake swimming, boat rentals, fishing, $11 to $16/night.

Take State Hwy. 20 south of Winthrop 3 miles, then follow Twin Lake Road west 2.3 miles to campground.

V) KLIPCHUCK FS CAMP

46 units, trailers to 32", stream, flush & pit toilets, wheelchair access, fishing, hiking, in Okanogan NF, $5/night (must buy pass in Twisp or Winthrop), information - (509) 826-3275..

Head northwest of Mazama 4 miles on State Hwy. 20, and take FSR 300 northwest 1.2 miles to camp.

W) LONE FIR FS CAMP

27 units, trailers to 22', piped & well water, pit toilets, creek, wheelchair access, fishing, view Silver Star Glacier, in Okanogan NF, $5/night (must buy pass in Twisp or Winthrop), information - (509) 826-3275..

Northwest of Mazama 11 miles on State Hwy. 20.

X) COLONIAL CREEK NCNP CAMP

164 campsites, trailers to 22' - no hookups, information - (360) 856-5700, wheelchair access, flush toilets, well water, picnic area, summer program, trailer waste disposal, at Diablo Lake, fishing, boat launch, hiking, in North Cascades National Park, pets okay, $10/night.

About 1.5 miles south of the Diablo Vista on State 20.

Y) NEWHALEM CREEK NCNP CAMP

129 campsites, trailers to 22', no hookups, flush toilets, wheelchair access, trailer waste disposal, on Skagit River, fishing, hiking, in North Cascades National Park, $10/night.

Southwest of Newhalem about 1 mile.

Z) CLARK'S SKAGIT RIVER COURT RV PARK

72 units, 38 w/full hookups, 20 w/water & elec., 6 w/out hookups, plus tent sites, reservation information - (360) 873-2250, showers, laundry, restaurant, on river, fishing, hiking, wildlife, pets okay, $12 to $25/night.

Located 6 miles east of Rockport on State Hwy. 20.

AA) H. MILLER STEELHEAD PARK

70 campsites, 60 w/water & electricity, plus 10 tent sites, information - (360) 853-8808, wheelchair access, picnic shelter, showers, playground, trailer waste disposal, river, swimming, fishing, boat launch, hiking, pets okay, $12 to $16/night.

At Rockport take Alfred Street to park.

BB) ROCKPORT STATE PARK

59 units, 50 w/full hookups, picnic shelter, wheelchair access includes old growth trail, trailer waste disposal, fishing, pets okay, $10 to $16/night.

Barely northwest of Rockport on State Hwy. 20.

CC) CREEKSIDE CAMPING

22 campsites, 10 w/full hookups, 10 w/water & electricity, plus 2 tent sites, pets okay, reservations - (360) 826-3566, showers, laundry, groceries, playground, trailer waste disposal, stream, fishing, $13 to $20/night.

Take State Hwy. 20 7 miles west of Concrete, and follow Baker Lake Road north .2 mile to campground.

DD) BURLINGTON/CASCADE KOA

120 campsites, 52 w/full hookups, 10 w/water & electricity, 18 w/electricity, plus 40 tent units, reservations - (360) 724-5511, wheelchair access, showers,

laundry, cable tv, propane, indoor pool, sauna, hot tubs, rec room, playfield, playground, trailer waste disposal, stream, fishing, $17 to $25/night.

At Burlington, take Cook Road to Old Highway 99 and head north 3.5 miles.

EE) RIVERBEND PARK

105 campsites, 75 w/full hookups, plus 30 tent units, information - (360) 428-4044, wheelchair access, showers, laundry, rec room, trailer waste disposal, river, fishing, $6 to $19/night.

Go south of Burlington on I-5 to exit #227 and take College Way west .01 mile to Freeway Drive. Campground is .5 mile north.

FF) BAYVIEW STATE PARK

78 units, 9 w/full hookups, community kitchen, on Padilla Bay, play area, $10 to $16/night.

Take State Hwy. 20 west of Burlington 6 miles; campground is 1.3 miles north of highway.

GG) DECEPTION PASS STATE PARK

246 units, some trailers - no hookups, information (360) 675-2417, community kitchen, wheelchair access, trailer waste disposal, boat launch, hiking, fishing, scuba diving area, swimming, pets okay, $10 to $11/night.

Deception State Park is located at the northern end of Whidbey Island, on State Hwy. 20.

HH) FORT EBEY STATE PARK

50 units, some trailers - no hookups, information (360) 678-4636, wheelchair accessible, beach access, hiking, scuba diving, fishing, $10 to $11/night.

Located on the west side of Whidbey Island, 6 miles northwest of Coupeville.

II) FORT CASEY STATE PARK

35 units, some trailers - no hookups, information (360) 678-4519, wheelchair access, explore old fort, hiking, boat launch, fishing, scuba diving, beach access, $10 to $11/night.

Take State Hwy. 20 south of Coupeville 3.5 miles, and drive west 4.5 miles.

JJ) SOUTH WHIDBEY STATE PARK

56 sites - no hookups, plus group camp, some trailers okay, information (360) 331-4559 - reservations (800) 452-5687, wheelchair access, trailer waste disposal, hiking, picnic area, scuba diving area, fishing, $10 to $11/night.

Leave Coupeville on State Hwy. 20 and follow State Hwy. 525 for 6 miles.

KK) SILVER SHORES RV PARK

110 units - 87 w/full hookups, 8 w/water & elec., plus 15 tent sites, reservations (425) 337-8741, showers, laundry, rec room, tennis, trailer waste disposal, small pets ok, on Silver Lake, swimming, fishing, $17 to $27/night.

In Everett, at 11621 W Silver Lake Rd.

There are over 100 campgrounds located along the Cascade Loop, and many more just off the main road. The campgrounds listed in this book are among the largest. If you are looking for a quieter, or more primitive campground, check the listings in *Free Campgrounds of Washington & Oregon* or *A Camper's Guide to Oregon & Washington*.

Vacation #3

High Mountain Trekking
in the Steens

Even the longest recreational vehicle will find the drive to Kiger Gorge fairly easy, and definitely worth the trip. This mountain was carved out by glaciers, and offers fantastic views.

FROM THE AUTHOR'S JOURNAL . . .

No matter how many times I visit the Steens Mountain area I am never disappointed, for the beauty never pales, even when measured against a memory.

This year, with the wildflowers in full bloom, I find myself looking out over mountain meadows with enough color to put a Van Gogh painting to shame. It's hard to imagine this land covered with glaciers, and the force with which they traveled, but the landscape they left behind gives silent testimony to their size and power.

Although we are here at a time when vacationers fill the roads elsewhere, this high mountain road is relatively empty. We pass only a few other kindred souls. Even though my daughter has spent nearly every one of her 16 summers camping the Pacific Northwest with me, this is the trip that leads her to say "Mom, when I have my own family we're going to spend all of our summers traveling just like this."

Our tour of the Malheur Wildlife Refuge was great. I let Jenica practice driving while I looked for wildlife. We must have stopped a hundred times to photograph deer resting along the creek, watch a flock of waterfowl, or to catch a better look at some small critter that had just run across the road. I've probably visited every wildlife refuge in the two-state area, but I always see more wildlife at Malheur than anywhere else.

Notes from a family vacation

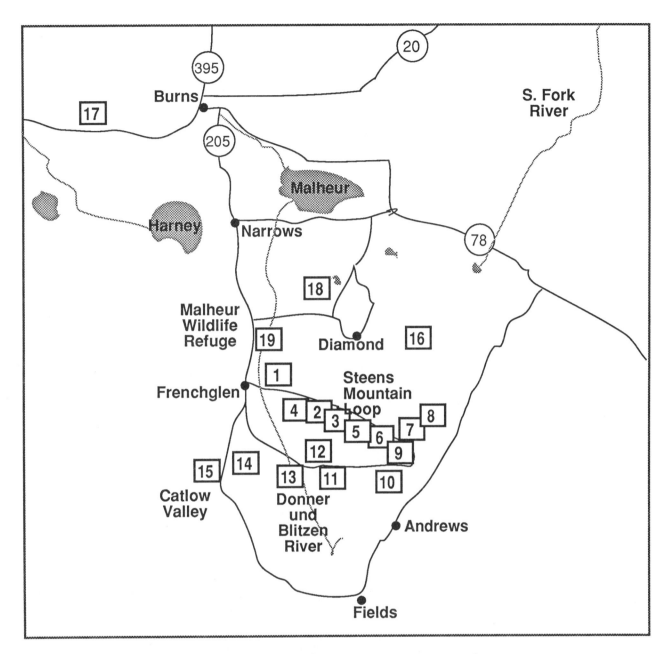

Steens Mountain Area Attractions

Oregon's highest road is located on Steens Mountain, 60 miles south of Burns. The Steens Mountain Loop provides stunning views of glacially carved gorges and the austere beauty of the high desert country.

Commonly referred to as "The Steens", this mountain was created 15 million years ago when a 30-mile-long fault block was shoved up through the cooling volcanic mass. The basalt mountain was drastically altered during the Ice Age, when mammoth glaciers gouged their way through its valleys. These glaciers left behind magnificent U-shaped gorges and a spectacular countryside.

Located within the Great Basin, the mountain's rugged eastern face towers high above the flat Alvord Desert. The western side makes a more gradual descent. It includes 775,600 acres, and has an elevation of 9,773 feet. About 70% of the mountain's land is managed by the BLM; 100,000 of those acres are classified recreational.

Traveling the Steens Mountain Loop

The **Steens Mountain Loop [1]** is a 66 mile unpaved roadway. Visitors should allow at least 4 hours to make the entire drive, but the scenery is so inviting that you might want to plan on an entire day. The road is not recommended for low clearance vehicles, RVs or trailers.

The upper road is closed from late October to mid-June; lower sections are generally open from late spring until winter snow falls. Parts of the loop are steep and narrow, but most cars have no problem along the lower portion. You'll find plenty of places to turn around if you decide the road has become too steep or rough for your vehicle.

Even if you only drive to Kiger Gorge Viewpoint, it's a worthwhile trip. The mountain scenery is spectacular. At 5,500 feet the landscape changes from a sagebrush dotted terrain to a rocky one filled with steep rimmed canyons.

The Aspen Belt, from 6,500 to 8,000 feet, is where you'll find groves of quaking aspen, mountain mahogany and isolated small meadows. The Alpine Bunchgrass Belt begins at 8,000 feet, and is the most sensational with its pris-

For the most part, the Steens Mountain Loop is fairly well-maintained, however rainstorms can leave it awfully muddy, so check the weather forecast before heading out.

Lily Lake, like hundreds of water-filled dips and hollows before it, will one day become entirely filled in by plants and sediment.

tine high country, open meadows and glaciated valleys. Summer temperatures here can drop into the low 20s at night; during the daytime they normally reach the 70s.

The North Loop Route

The northern portion of the Steens Mountain Loop begins at Frenchglen, near Page Springs Campground. It will lead you past Lily, Fish, Page and Honeymoon Lakes, by Whorehouse Meadows, and along the head of Kiger Gorge for some spectacular views.

A few mountain lakes are all that remain of the ancient glaciers and numerous ice fields that once covered this land. Over the centuries, most of the glacially created lakes have disappeared, filled in by plants and sediment. A lot of the meadows you see along the way were once lakes. **Lily Lake [2]**, near the beginning of the loop drive, is a living example of how those lakes were consumed.

Fish Lake [3], just a few miles past Lily, is a glacial pocket at 7,000 feet. It is stocked with rainbow and eastern brook cutthroat trout. Located just off the road, it's one of the two lakes here that are large enough to support fish. Several mountain streams offer year round trout fishing.

Corral Creek [4], Honeymoon Lake [5] and **Whorehouse Meadows [6]** date back to the Roaring Twenties, a time when local cowboys, and Basque and Irish sheepherders, brought their livestock up to summer on the mountain's cooler pastures. The aspen groves found here were where the men gathered for music and revelry. It is said that more than 100,000 animals grazed the mountain during that time; today only 10,000 cattle are allowed.

The **Kiger Gorge Overlook [7]** provides a view that includes the Alvord Basin. If you're uneasy about driving the entire loop road, this is a good place to turn around.

The **"Big Nick" [8]**, located between Kiger Gorge and House Creek, is the only place on the main rim that has been completely eroded away. This area sports a number of small lakes where glaciers once sat.

This is where the road starts getting rougher, but it offers spectacular views of the **Little Blitzen River [9]**, and a chance to explore Little Blitzen and Big Indian Canyons.

To reach **Wildhorse Lake (10)**, walk down the dirt road located just past Little Blitzen Gorge. Wildhorse is situated in a hanging valley, and stocked with Lahontan cutthroat trout. This oasis was created by a second series of glaciers which formed at the top of the gorge,

and pushed fresh earth down the basalt landscape. When they melted, they left this beautiful isolated valley behind.

The South Loop Route

Big Indian [11] and **Little Blitzen Gorge [12]** were once filled with rivers of ice. The road winds along a narrow ridge that separates the canyons from the mountain's sheer eastern face, then takes you along the hogback that separates the two rivers, takes you down the face of another fault, and travels below the Rooster Comb.

The mountain's **Donner und Blitzen River [13]** has been designated wild and scenic. Its protected waters include Fish Creek, and the creeks running down Little Blitzen and Big Indian Gorge.

Continuing on, you will encounter several more scenic viewpoints before making your way down the mountain to **Catlow Valley [14]** and State Highway 205. You rejoin the highway 10 miles south of Frenchglen.

The Steens are home to lots of wildlife, so be sure to bring your binoculars. Bighorn sheep frequent the east rim, mule deer and Rocky Mountain elk are also easy to spot, particularly at dawn and dusk.

Pronghorn antelope, America's fastest mammal, graze on the mountain. They prefer the sagebrush of the lower elevation, but it's not uncommon to see them near the top.

Wild horses frequent the plateau between **Catlow Rim [15]** and the Blitzen River. The herd includes about

300 horses, and is monitored by the BLM to preserve their free-roaming spirit. Coyotes, bobcats, mountain lions, black-tailed jackrabbits and beaver also live on the mountain.

Golden eagles, hawks, and falcons soar overhead in search of food, riding the rim's wind currents. Sage grouse, mourning dove, quail, chukar partridge, owls and songbirds are all plentiful. You'll find the best birdwatching in the alpine uplands.

In the early summer the mountain landscape is bright with wildflowers. They begin to bloom in April at lower elevations, and by the time those start to fade, flowers begin appearing at higher elevations. Along the high road wildflowers blossom into mid-summer. The colors of fall too are grand here, especially in the Aspen Belt.

Low Elevation Attractions

You can also drive clear around the mountain's base for a different perspective of The Steens. To do this, follow State Highway 205 to Frenchglen, take the county road through Catlow Valley, Fields and Andrews, and then follow State Highway 78 back to 205.

There's a lot more to a Steens Mountain vacation than just seeing the mountain. You can watch the wild mustang herd that grazes southeast of Diamond, or take a tour of the BLM wild horse corrals west of Burns. Visit Diamond Craters for a look at North America's largest variety of basaltic volcanic features, or enjoy lunch at the historic Frenchglen Hotel before an afternoon in the Malheur National Wildlife Refuge.

To reach the **Kiger Mustang Viewing Area [16]**, take State Highway 205 north of Frenchglen to the turnoff for Diamond. Follow this road past the town, and on up the grade. At the top, turn right where the sign points to an unimproved road and drive 11 miles to where the wild mustangs graze.

When these herds get too large for the range, some are captured and placed for adoption through the BLM Adopt-A-Horse Program. These animals are tamed at the BLM **wild horse corrals [17]** on the north side of US Highway 20, west of Burns. Stop in at the BLM office for permission to visit the corrals. (The corrals were torched in December of 1997 but are scheduled to be rebuilt.)

Diamond Craters [18] is where you'll find a variety of unusual lava formations. To get there, take the Diamond turnoff and follow the signs. There are no tourist facilities along this paved road, so check the gas gauge before you leave. The BLM offers a self-guided tour brochure to help you explore the domes, craters and other features of Diamond Craters.

If you like wildlife, you'll definitely want to spend some time at the **Malheur National Wildlife Refuge [19]**. Mule deer and ducks are easy to spot along the Donner und Blitzen Canal; coyote, raccoon, weasel, mink, badger, porcupine, muskrat and jackrabbits are also common.

Herons, vultures, hawks, falcon, eagles, owls, songbirds, and a variety of waterfowl are all regular visitors. If you keep your eyes peeled, you might also see

Volcanic attractions are plentiful, and easy to explore, in Oregon's southeast corner. Diamond Craters, shown here, is easily visible from the road. These remains take many shapes; here it resembles a buckled parking lot.

white pelican, cormorant, snowy egrets, whistling and trumpeter swans, or sandhill cranes. This wetland area has been a major nesting place, and migratory stopover, since prehistoric times.

The little museum at the refuge headquarters is a favorite with kids of all ages. It provides an opportunity for them to examine stuffed birds, nests and eggs up close.

A tour of Steens Mountain is a good way to get in touch with the state's earliest beginnings. From prehistoric volcanoes and glaciers to 19th century sheep and cattle ranching, it's easy to see that it all happened here.

For Additional Information

A phone call to the Burns area Bureau of Land Management (BLM) office will get you lots of information on this area. Be sure to ask for the Diamond Craters self-guided tour brochure as well as information on the Steens Mountain Loop.

BLM – Burns Office
(541) 573-4400

Malheur Wildlife Refuge
(541) 493-2612

Burns/Harney County Chamber of Commerce
(541) 573-2636

Steens Mountain Area Accommodations

BURNS

Bontemps Motel (800) 229-1394
74 W Monroe (541) 573-2037
15 rooms - some 1-2 bedroom suites,
some w/kitchenettes, limited handicap
access, sign language inter., concierge,
garage parking, pets okay - $3 fee,
located downtown, $27-50.

Lone Pine Guest Ranch
51 Lone Pine Rd. (541) 573-2103
2 rooms w/baths, kitchenettes & fireplaces, some pets - call for details,
handicap access, working ranch -
horse corrals avail., animal petting
area in summer, $55-75,

Orbit Motel (800) 235-6155
Jct. of Hwys. 20/395N (541) 573-2034
31 units, 5 w/kitchenettes, pets okay,
outdoor pool, $28-40.

Ponderosa Best Western
(800) 303-2047 or (541) 573-2047
577 W. Monroe
52 rooms, pets okay - $10 fee, 1 room
is handicap accessible, outdoor pool,
located downtown - there is a restaurant next door, $47-85.

Royal Inn (541) 573-1700
999 Oregon Ave.
38 rooms, 2 are handicap accessible,
pets okay - $25 fee, indoor pool, spa &
sauna, nearby restaurant, $38-66.

Sage Country Inn (541) 573-7243
351-1/2 W Monroe
Private rooms w/baths, no pets. This
bed & breakfast is housed in a 1907
Colonial home, seasonal, $50-75.

Silver Spur Motel (800) 400-2077
789 Broadway (541) 573-2077
26 units w/microwave & refrigerator,
$36-60, pets okay - $5/night, free use
of nearby health club, located downtown, Visa/MC.

DIAMOND

McCoy Creek Inn (541) 493-2131
Diamond Junction Road
3 rooms in a turn-of-century home
plus sleeping quarters in the
bunkhouse, private bathrooms, outdoor hot tub, no pets or smoking
allowed, limited handicap access, $75,
not open year round.

FRENCHGLEN

Frenchglen Historic Hotel
(541) 493-2825
State Hwy. 205 in Frenchglen
This historic hotel is a State Heritage
Site. It offers sleeping rooms w/shared
baths in a 1916 hotel/wayside, and
includes an on-site family-style restaurant. Unique & quiet setting, $48-50,
not open year round.

Steens Mountain Resort
(541) 493-2415
In Frenchglen - on Hwy. 205
This campground/resort is located
just beyond the Frenchglen Hotel. It
offers 5 modular cabins w/kitch-
enettes for $49-55. Located near the
river, you can go swimming, fishing or
hiking. They offer limited groceries,
but you can walk to the Frenchglen
Hotel restaurant (reservations are a
good idea at the restaurant).

Steens Mountain Area Campgrounds & RV Parks

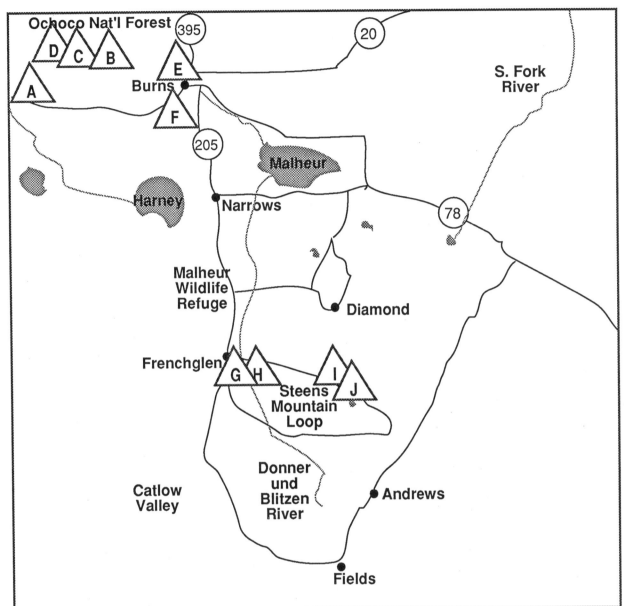

A) CHICKAHOMINY BLM RECREATION SITE

Open camp area, vault toilets - wheelchair accessible, drinking water, firepits w/grills, picnic tables, lake fishing, boating - lake's water level varies by season, boat ramp, wildlife viewing, open April thru September, $4/night.

Located west of Burns 34 miles on US Highway 20.

B) FALLS FS CAMP

5 campsites, trailers to 22', well water, pit toilets, stream fishing, in Ochoco NF, pets okay, $4/night.

Located northwest of Burns. Follow FSR 47 for 15 miles before turning onto FSR 41. You will follow this road for an additional 18 miles to Falls Campground.

C) EMIGRANT FS CAMP

6 units, trailers to 22', well water - not always drinkable, pit toilets, stream fishing, in Ochoco NF, no overnight fee.

Follow FSR 47 northwest for 15 miles before turning onto FSR 41. You will follow this road an additional 20 miles to the campground.

D) DELINTMENT LAKE FS CAMP

24 units, trailers to 32', picnic area, well water, pit toilets – handicap accessible, wheelchair accessible fishing dock, boat launch, boating, fishing, in Ochoco NF, pets okay, elev. 5600', $6/night.

Follow FSR 47 northwest for 15 miles, then FSR 41 an additional 30 miles to the lake and campground.

E) VILLAGE RV PARK

41 campsites w/full hookups, no tents allowed, reservations - (541) 573-7640, showers, laundry, nearby fishing, small dogs okay - limit 2, $20/night.

Located in Burns, just off US Hwy. 395/20, at 1273 Seneca Drive.

F) SANDS TRAILER PARK

16 campsites, 10 w/full hookups, plus 6 tent units, pull-thrus, information - (541) 573-7010, showers, located across from golf course, $10/night.

This campground is located 1 mile south of Burns on US Hwy. 395/20.

G) STEENS MOUNTAIN RESORT CAMP & CAMPER CORRAL

90 campsites, 45 w/full hookups, 45 w/water & electricity, plus large tent area, reservation information - (541) 493-2415, fire pits, showers, laundry, trailer waste disposal, river, swimming, fishing, hiking, elev. 4100', $10 to $15/night.

Located just beyond Frenchglen Hotel.

H) PAGE SPRINGS BLM CAMP

36 units, trailers to 24', drinking water, pit toilets, fire pits w/grills, picnic tables, grey water station, wildlife viewing, hiking, borders on Malheur Wildlife Refuge, fishing, elev. 4339', open year round - host in summer, $4/night.

Located 4 miles southeast of Frenchglen, on the Blitzen River.

I) FISH LAKE BLM CAMP

23 units, trailers to 24', well water, pit toilets - wheelchair accessible, fire pits w/grills, picnic tables, grey water station, wildlife viewing, lake - no motors allowed - stocked w/trout, hiking trails, boat dock, boating, swimming, small horse corral, elev. 7500', open July thru October - host in summer, $4/night.

Located 17 miles east of Frenchglen, on the northern portion of the Steens Mountain Loop Road.

J) JACKMAN BLM PARK

6 units, drinking water, pit toilet - wheelchair accessible, fire pits w/grills, picnic tables, grey water station, hiking, bird watching, elev. 8100', open July thru October, $4/night.

Located 20 miles east of Frenchglen on the northern portion of the Steens Mountain Loop Road.

J) SOUTH STEENS BLM PARK

21 units - 15 w/horse hitches, drinking water, pit toilet - wheelchair accessible, fire pits w/grills, picnic tables, grey water station, wildlife viewing, hiking & horse trails, horse ramp, nearby fishing, elev. 5300', open May thru October - host in summer, $4/night.

Located 28 miles east of Frenchglen on the northern portion of the Steens Mountain Loop Road - near the Donner und Blitzen River.

If the BLM campgrounds are full, you can generally camp elsewhere, as long as you don't drive off the road, stay out of areas that are posted closed, and practice "no trace" camping so that no one will be able to tell you were there after you leave.

Vacation #4

Kites, Sunken Ships, Old Forts and the World's Longest Beach

The Long Beach Peninsula is a popular with kids of all ages, especially those who enjoy kite flying. It's also a great place for beachcombing, long hikes and frisbee.

FROM THE AUTHOR'S JOURNAL · · ·

As the music began playing over the loud speakers, eight kites moved upward, flipped over, and turned right with the beat. Each duplicated the movements of its neighbor with the precision of a military marching unit. Several minutes later, the music ended and, as it did, all eight kites came to rest on the beach in a perfectly straight line.

We gazed upward for the next two days, watching one beautifully choreographed performance after another as kite enthusiasts from near and far competed in Washington's annual international kite festival. The bright colors, interesting shapes, and seemingly effortless team-work were memorable.

I had visited the Long Beach Peninsula countless times in the past, but always before, it had been to enjoy the seemingly endless ocean beaches. We spent very little time walking the beach on this trip. I knew that the beaches would be there next week, but this unusual festi-val would not happen again for another year.

Of course we did manage to squeeze in a visit to Marsh's Museum. This is one Long Beach attraction my family has to visit every time we're in town. Its eclectic collection of whimsy, antiques and souvenirs never gets boring. Pushing coins into the old-fashioned music machines, we are instantly transported to a time when things were built to last, as we watch and listen to the world's first juke-boxes.

Notes from a Washington coast weekend

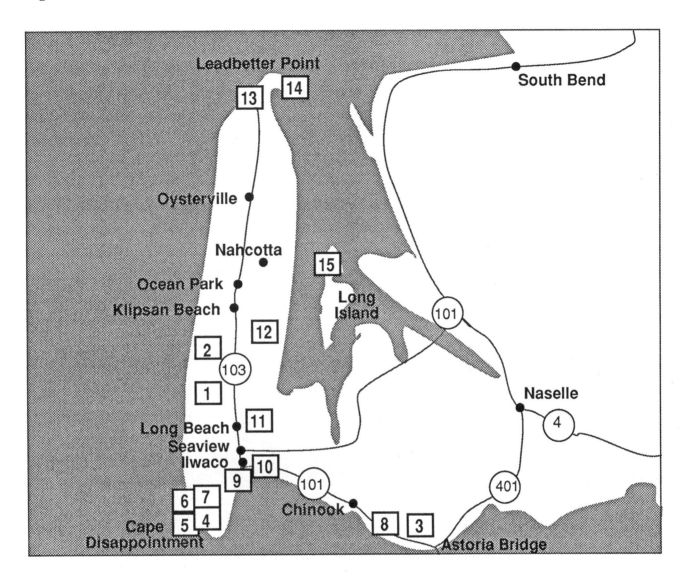

Long Beach Peninsula Area Attractions

Kite-flying is a popular pastime with Long Beach Peninsula visitors, making it a great place for a family vacation. Almost any time of year, the skies are filled with bright colors and interesting shapes.

The peninsula's steady breezes have made it the location of a special event for kite enthusiasts since 1981. Held in mid August, the **Washington State International Kite Festival [1]** draws competitors from all over the world for seven days of activities.

Brightly colored kite trains, lighted stunt kites, and an array of one-of-a-kind, box, and handcrafted kites crowd the skies. Workshops for beginning and advanced flyers are offered, along with daily demonstrations. On the final day, there's a Festival of Kites, an attempt to break the Western Hemisphere record for the most kites in the sky at once.

The treacherous waters off Cape Disappointment have been swallowing up boats for nearly three centuries, earning it the nickname of *the graveyard of the Pacific.*

The Long Beach Peninsula is also where you'll find the **world's longest beach [2]**. Its 28-mile length gives visitors unlimited ocean access. Camping is not allowed on the beach, but campers will find plenty of places to stay on the peninsula.

Washington's ocean beaches are considered highways, which means you can drive most of the peninsula's shoreline. Follow the same rules you would on any other state highway. Be sure to keep your car below the high tide line, on the wet sand; driving on higher ground will get your vehicle stuck in the soft sand.

The waters off the Long Beach Peninsula are littered with sunken ships; hundreds have disappeared here during the past 270 years. In fact, this area is known as 'the graveyard of the Pacific'. Schooners, sloops, steamers, trollers, brigs, gunboats and other ships have been lost to its treacherous currents.

Exploring the Peninsula's Historic Beginnings

When Captain Gray landed on the north shore of the Columbia River in 1792, his visit launched the American claim to the northwest coast. Lewis and Clark arrived in November of 1805, and reported this area as being inhabited by Chief Comcomally and his tribe. They lived in communal long houses along the Columbia River and the peninsula's Willapa Bay.

You can visit the **Lewis and Clark Expedition Campsite [3]**. A marker near St. Mary's Church, along the Columbia River just west of the Astoria bridge, identifies this historic spot. A second monument in Long Beach, at State Highway 103 and Third Street, marks the most northwestern point visited by the expedition.

The **Lewis and Clark Interpretive Center [4]** at Fort Canby State Park focuses on the group's 8,000-mile jour-

ney, painting a vivid picture of the people involved and the hardships they suffered. There is currently no charge to tour the center, and it is handicap-accessible. Open daily throughout the summer, the rest of the year it operates on weekends only, from 9:00 a.m. to 5:00 p.m.

This is also a good place to learn about the cape's two lighthouses, and Fort Canby. The **Cape Disappointment [5]** and **North Head Lighthouses [6]** are still standing, and were built in 1856 and 1899.

Fort Canby [7] was the state's first coastal defense installation, and was in active use from 1875 to 1957. Kids will

Fort Canby served as a coastal defense station from 1875 to 1957. War buffs and kids of all ages will enjoy exploring its now-deserted bunkers.

enjoy exploring the fort's old bunkers. The interpretive center sits on the site of two of the original defense batteries, and has a view of Cape Disappointment; the same one early explorers had when they first sighted the Pacific Ocean.

Fort Canby State Park's 2,000 acres provide hiking trails, picnic facilities, campsites, ocean access, birdwatching, and whale watching. Salmon, rock cod, ling cod, flounder, perch and sea bass are caught in the surrounding waters.

The waters off Cape Disappointment are dangerous, and swimming there is unsafe. Fort Canby's Waikiki Beach is probably the safest spot, but be careful and stay close to shore. During the winter, storms bring huge green waves crashing over the rocks of Cape Disappointment, shooting water a hundred feet into the air.

Fort Columbia [8] was built around 1897 and remains in near-original condition. It now serves as a state park, providing visitors with the opportunity to see what military life was like in the U.S. Army's coastal artillery corps around the turn of the century.

You can explore military bunkers, batteries and lookouts, and tour some of the 14 wooden buildings. These include a guardhouse, barracks, hospital and supply building. The displays and museum exhibits are fun and educational.

Fort Columbia State Park is two miles west of the Astoria Bridge, on US Highway 101. You can explore the grounds daily during the summer; they are closed on Mondays and Tuesdays the balance of the year.

Things To Do, Places To Go
Visit the **Ilwaco boat basin [9]**, and you'll see tuna boats, trawlers, shrimpers, salmon trollers, crabbers, and charter boats. It's an exciting place to be when the boats come in with the day's catch. Dockside canneries sell fresh seafood, and many welcome visitors.

If you'd like to learn more about local history, visit the **Ilwaco Heritage Museum [10]** on Lake Street. You'll find it open from 9:00 a.m. to 4:00 p.m. Monday through Saturday, and noon to 4:00 p.m. on Sunday.

The museum's most popular exhibit is a 50-foot-long miniature railroad. An exact replica of the 1920 Ilwaco Railroad and Navigation Company's local line, its landscape includes exact copies of local buildings and thousands of tiny trees. Other museum exhibits highlight local Indians, pioneer life, the fur trade, and coastal explorers.

The town of Long Beach is popular with families. It has an amusement center, go-karts, bumper cars, kiddie rides, lots of interesting shops, and **Marsh's Free Museum [11]**.

Marsh's is best described as a combination side show, antique game room, second-hand store, gift shop. You'll find freak-show oddities that include two-headed animals, Jake the alligator man, shrunken heads, and an array of bizarre man-made creatures.

You can operate antique juke boxes, peep shows and old-time game machines. Even small children, and peo-

Fort Columbia was built around 1897, and is in near-original condition. It has been preserved as a state park, and is open to the public.

ple who think museums are boring, will spend hours at Marsh's.

A series of brightly painted murals decorate the buildings of Ilwaco, Long Beach, Chinook and Nahcotta. They depict turn-of-the-century street scenes, farming, fishing, cranberry harvests, and other historic events. These huge outdoor canvasses bring color and artistry to the towns.

Driving towards the peninsula's north end, you'll find **Loomis Lake State Park** [12] just past Cranberry Road. Loomis Lake is the largest of the numerous lakes that occupy the peninsula's center. Trumpeter Swans nest here in the winter; summer brings trout anglers, canoeists, and picnickers.

Leadbetter Point State Park [13], on the peninsula's northern tip, is popular with birdwatchers. Over 100 species of birds visit this refuge, including black brandt and snowy plover. Other park activities include surf fishing, digging for clams, beachcombing, and hiking along dune and forest trails. The open dune area at the very tip is part of the **Willapa National Wildlife Refuge [14]**.

Long Island [15], in Willapa Bay, is also part of the wildlife refuge. This island is probably best known as the site of the United States' last stand of old-growth red cedar.

You'll need your own boat to reach the island. Cross the channel at Nahcotta and you'll find a 2.5-mile trail leading to the 274-acre grove of ancient trees. These trees range in diameter from five to eleven feet and have an average height of 160 feet.

Long Island is also the Pacific Coast's largest estuarine island. Natural inhabitants include deer, bear, elk, beaver, otter, and a variety of birds. Canoeing, kayaking, hiking, birdwatching and limited camping are available. Visitors need to take their own water with them, and pack out everything they pack in.

Camping on Long Island is only for those who respect nature, and is restricted to a handful of established campsites. High tide plays an important role in campground accessibility, so check with the Willapa Wildlife Refuge officials before assuming you'll find a place to pitch your tent.

For Additional Information

If you want to plan your trip to coincide with one of the many area festivals, check with the Visitors Bureau. They can provide information on a number of fun happenings. Most offer a variety of family activities, and focus on local products. Popular events include an annual sand-sculpture contest, garlic festival, and the WA International Kite Festival.

**Long Beach Peninsula
Visitors Bureau**
(800) 451-2542

Lewis & Clark Interpretive Center
(360) 642-3078

Fort Canby State Park
(360) 642-3078

Fort Columbia State Park
(360) 777-8221

Willapa National Wildlife Refuge
(360) 484-3482

Long Beach Peninsula Area Accommodations

ILWACO

Chick-A-Dee Inn
(888) 244-2523 or (360) 642-8686
120 Williams St. NE
8 rooms w/baths plus suite, old church, $99-180 ($76-150).

Heidi's Inn
(360) 642-2387
126 E Spruce (US Hwy. 101)
25 rooms, some w/kitchens, $5 pet fee, indoor spa, near boat basin, $45-70 ($30-65).

Kola House B&B
(360) 642-2819
211 Pearl Ave.
5 rooms w/baths, suite w/sauna, overlooks port, $65-75.

Motel 101 Haciendas
(360) 642-8459
101 Brumbach @ US Hwy. 101
8 rooms, some w/kitchens, no pets, $30-60 ($30-50).

LONG BEACH

Anchorage Court
(800) 646-2351 or (360) 642-2351
2209 N Boulevard
9 rooms w/kitchens, pets okay, ocean front, handicap access, nearby golf, $69-113 ($59-103).

Arcadia Court
(360) 642-2613
401 N Boulevard
8 rooms, some w/kitchens, some, pets - call - $10 fee, 3 blocks to beach, $42-86 ($38-79).

Boardwalk Cottages
(800) 569-3804 or (360) 642-2305
800 Ocean Blvd. S
4 rooms plus 6 cabins, some w/kitchens, no pets, non-smoking, $72-100 ($52-80).

Boreas B&B
(888) 642-8069 or (360) 642-8069
607 N Boulevard
3 suites w/baths plus 2 rooms/shared bath, ocean view, near boardwalk, $100-130 ($95-125).

Boulevard Motel
(360) 642-2434
301 N Boulevard
14 rooms plus 8 cabins, kitchens, pets okay, indoor pool, handicap access, walk to beach,$50-85 ($40-65).

Chatauqua Lodge
(800) 869-8401 or (360) 642-4401
304 N 14th
180 rooms & suites, ocean front & honeymoon suites, some w/jacuzzi & lots w/kitchens, $8 pet fee, indoor pool, sauna, handicap access, beach access, $55-160 ($40-115).

Edgewater Inn
(800) 561-2456 or (360) 642-2311
409 10th St. SW
84 rooms, pets okay, rest/lounge, handicap access, ocean view, $64-104 ($49-89).

Edgewood Inn
(800) 460-7196 or (360) 642-8227
112 8th St. NE
3 rooms plus suite, non-smoking, close to ocean, $65-$95.

Land's End On Ocean
(360) 642-8268
13003 "N" Alley
2 rooms w/baths, private path to beach, $105-120.

Long Beach Motel
(360) 642-3500
1200 Pacific Hwy. S
9 rooms plus 4 cabins - some w/kitchens, $15 pet fee, $49-99 ($30-80).

Ocean Lodge
(360) 642-5400
208 Bolstad
65 rooms plus 3 cabins w/kitchens,
some of the rooms have kitchenettes,
pets okay, outdoor pool, sauna, ocean
view, handicap access, $50-100 ($45-
90).

Our Place at the Beach
(800) 538-5107 or (360) 642-3793
1309 S Boulevard
25 rooms plus 2 cabins w/kitchens,
pets okay - fee is $5-10 depending on
the size of the pet, sauna & steam
room plus an exercise room, ocean
view, $45-75 ($37-70).

Pacific View Motel
(800) 238-0859 or (360) 642-2415
203 Bolstad
2 motel rooms plus 9 cabins
w/kitchens, located on beach, $62-
100 ($42-78).

Sand-Lo Motel
(800) 676-2601 or (360) 642-2600
1910 N Pacific
10 rooms, small pets okay - $5 pet fee,
nearby restaurant, beach access, $45-
65 ($42-54).

Scandinavian Gardens
(800) 988-9277
1610 California Ave. S
4 rooms plus 1 suite - all with private
baths, spa & sauna, $95-135.

Shaman Motel
(800) 753-3750 or (360) 642-3714
115 3rd St. SW
42 rooms, many units have a kitchenette, pets okay - $5 fee, seasonal
outdoor pool, beach access, $54-94
($49-69).

Super 8 Motel
(800) 800-8000 or (360) 642-8988
500 Ocean Blvd.
50 rooms, no pets allowed, handicap
accessible rooms - please inquire
ahead of time, $79-102 ($49-69).

The Breakers
(800) 288-8890 or (360) 642-4414
State Hwy. 103 @ N 26th
114 rooms, 1 & 2 bedroom suites,
many w/kitchens, view & fireplace
rooms, $10 pet fee, indoor pool, hot
tub, handicap access, walk to beach,
$74-192 ($59-171).

NAHCOTTA

Moby Dick Hotel & Oyster Farm
(360) 665-4543
Sandridge Road @ Willapa Bay
10 rooms in charming 1929 vintage
hotel, includes full breakfast, sauna,
on Willapa Bay, $60-85.

Our House in Nahcotta B&B
(360) 665-6667
268th & Dell
2 suites w/personal parlors and baths
in Cape Cod style home, includes continental plus breakfast, walk to
Willapa Bay & Ark Restaurant, $95.

OCEAN PARK

Blackwood Beach Cottage
(888) 376-6356 or (360) 665-6356
20711 Pacific Way
2 suites plus 8 cabins w/kitchens, no
smoking, no pets, beach access, $80-
139 ($75-$125).

Caswell's on Bay
(888) 553-2319 or (360) 665-6535
25204 Sandridge Rd.
5 rooms w/baths, $95-150.

Coastal Watch B&B
(360) 665-6774
1511 264th Place
2 smoke-free rooms w/baths, picnic
area w/BBQ, walk to beach, $95.

Coastal Cottages (800) 200-0424
In Ocean Park (360) 665-4658
4 cottages w/kitchens, pets okay, walk
to beach, $59-$69 ($50-$60).

DoveShire B&B
(888) 553-2320 or (360) 665-3017
21914 Pacific Way
4 Gothic suites w/baths, $100.

Klipsan Beach Cottage
(360) 665-4888
22617 Pacific Hwy.
10 cabins w/kitchens, no pets, ocean view, $80-$150 ($70-$125).

Ocean Park Resort
(800) 835-4634 or (360) 665-4585
25904 "R" St.
12 rooms plus 3 cabins, kitchens, pets - $5 fee, outdoor pool, handicap access, $60-$100.

Sunset View Resort
(800) 272-9199 or (360) 665-4494
256th & Park
54 rooms - some w/kitchen, pets okay, ball courts, hot tub, sauna, ocean views, $65-185.

Westgate Motor Court
(360) 665-4211
20803 Pacific Hwy.
6 cabins w/kitchens, pets okay, beach access, $48-65.

Whalebone House
(888) 298-3330 or (360) 665-5371
2101 Bay Ave.
4 rooms w/private baths in 1889 Victorian, includes full breakfast, no kids, no pets, no smoking, located near bay, $85-99 ($75-89).

OCEAN SHORES

Best Western Lighthouse Suites Inn
(800) 757-SURF or (360) 289-2311
491 Damon Rd. NW
76 rooms w/fireplace, ref./microwave, ocean view, inc. cont. breakfast, spa units, indoor pool, laundry, handicap accessible units, $100-175 ($65-157).

Canterbury Inn
(800) 562-6678 or (360) 289-3317
643 Ocean Shores Blvd.
44 studios & 1-2 bedroom suites w/kitchens, on beach, pool, hot tub, exercise room, laundry, $82-170.

Days Inn
(360) 289-9570
891 Ocean Shores Blvd.
Spacious rooms w/ref. & microwave, inc. cont. breakfast, indoor pool & spa, walk to beach & restaurants, $54-89.

Gitche Gumee Motel
(800) 448-2433 or (360) 289-3323
648 Ocean Shores Blvd.
80 rooms & 3 bedroom suites w/fireplaces, some kitchen units, indoor & outdoor pool, saunas, ocean view, walk to restaurant, $45-165.

Grey Gull Motel
(800) 562-9712 or (360) 289-3381
Ocean Shores Blvd.
Rooms - 1-2 bedroom suites & penthouse, some kitchen units, ocean views, fireplaces, microwaves, year round pool, hot tub, indoor sauna, pets okay, $98-268 ($70-215).

SEAVIEW

Lion's Paw B&B
(360) 642-2481
3310 Pacific Hwy.
4 rooms w/baths, built in 1900, hot tub, $70-90.

Seaview CoHo Motel
(800) 681-8153 or (360) 642-2531
3707 Pacific Way
13 rooms plus 2 cabins, some kitchens, pets okay, $55-110 ($30-80).

Shelburne Country Inn
(800) INN-1896 or (360) 642-2442
4415 Pacific Way
15 rooms w/baths, built in 1896, $109-179 ($102-172).

Sou'Wester Lodge
(360) 642-2542
Beach Access Road
3 rooms w/shared bath & kitchen in 1892 historic lodge plus homey cedar cabins and a collection of whimsical mobile homes & RVs w/bath & kitchen facilities, simple comforts & pleasant atmosphere for non-traditional people, ocean views, pets okay, walk to shops & restaurant, $39-109.

Long Beach Peninsula Campgrounds & RV Parks

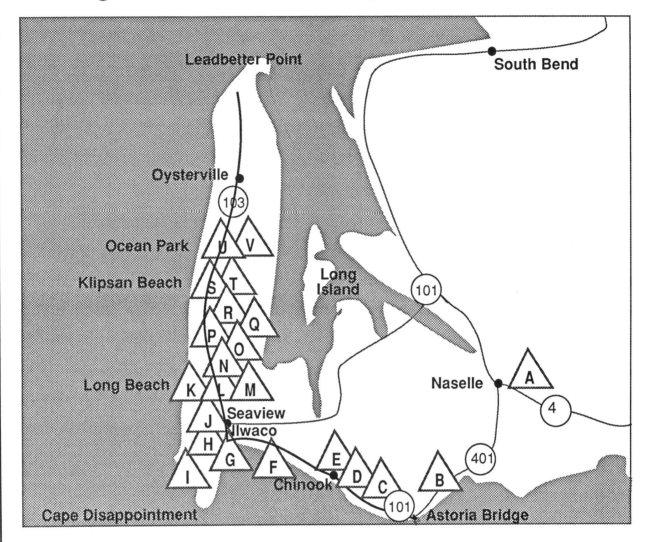

A) NASELLE TRAILER COURT

24 trailer sites w/full hookups, no tents, reservations (360) 484-3351, showers, laundry, $15/night - seniors $10.

Northeast of Ilwaco. Take US Hwy. 101 southeast 10 miles, State 401 north 12 miles, and State Hwy. 4 east 1.5 miles to #1061.

B) CHINOOK BAIT/TACKLE & RV

100 units, 75 w/water & electricity plus grassy tent area, reservations (360) 777-8475, showers, laundry, trailer waste disposal, picnic area, near river, small pets okay, $12 to $16/night.

Take State 401 3 miles north of its junction with US Hwy. 101.

C) MAUCH'S SUNDOWN RV PARK

50 campsites, 40 w/full hookups plus 10 w/water & electricity, tents okay, reservations (360) 777-8713, showers, propane, laundry, trailer waste disposal, on river, fishing, $8 to $15/night.

Located just west of the Astoria Bridge, on US Hwy. 101.

D) RIVER'S END RV

100 campsites - 20 w/full hookups, 40 w/water & electricity, plus 40 grassy

tent sites, reservations (360) 777-8317, showers, laundry, rec room, playground, trailer waste disposal, river, fishing, $14 to $18/night.

Located just south of Chinook, on US Hwy. 101.

E) ILWACO KOA

200 campsites, 36 w/full hookups, 90 w/elec. only, plus 74 tent units, reservations (360) 642-3292, showers, laundry, groceries, trailer waste disposal, playground, rec room, ocean access, fishing, $20 to $26/night.

Located on US Hwy. 101, between Ilwaco and Chinook.

F) THE BEACON RV PARK

60 campsites - 40 w/full hookups, plus 20 w/electricity only, reservation information (360) 642-2138, no tents, showers, cable tv, river, fishing, pets okay, $18 to $20/night.

In Ilwaco, at east end of docks.

G) COVE RV PARK

43 units w/full hookups (6 are pull-thrus), some tent sites, pets welcome, reservations (360) 642-3689, showers, laundry, trailer waste disposal, by Baker Bay, $15/night.

In Ilwaco, at west end of port area.

H) FORT CANBY STATE PARK

254 units, 60 w/full hookups, wheelchair access, groceries, trailer waste disposal, boat launch, fishing, interpretive center, ocean access, trails, $10 to $16/night.

Located 2.5 miles southwest of Ilwaco.

I) WILDWOOD RV PARK

30 units w/full hookups, tents okay, reservations (360) 642-2131, private lake, picnic area, showers, volleyball & basketball courts, horseshoe pit, boat parking, walk to restaurant & shops, $15 to $17/night.
In Seaview, at 5415 Sandridge Road.

J) SOU'WESTER LODGE & TRAILER PARK

50 campsites w/full hookups, tenters welcome, reservation information (360) 642-2542, showers, laundry, ocean access, fishing, $16-26/night.

Leave US Hwy. 101 just south of Seaview, on Seaview Beach Road, and head west 1 block to park.

K) SAND CASTLE RV PARK

38 campsites w/full hookups, no tents, reservations (360) 642-2174, showers, laundry, ocean access, $18 to $23/night.

In Long Beach, right on State Hwy. 103.

L) ANTHONY'S HOME COURT

25 campsites w/full hookups, reservations (360) 642-2802, showers, laundry, fish cleaning area, $15 to $18/night.

In Long Beach, at 1310 Pacific Hwy. N.

M) DRIFTWOOD RV PARK

56 campsites w/full hookups - some are pull thrus, group facilities, reservations (360) 642-2711, showers, cable tv, laundry, picnic table area, nearby ocean access, pets okay, fishing, $18/night.

In Long Beach, right on State Hwy. 103.

M) OCEANIC RV PARK

20 units w/full hookups, no tents, reservations (360) 642-3836, pets okay, showers, picnic area, beach access, $15/night.

In Long Beach, at South 5th & Pacific.

M) PIONEER RV PARK

34 units - all w/full hookups, grassy tent area, reservations (360) 642-3990, pets okay, showers, beach access, walk to store & restaurant, $15 to $17/night.

In Long Beach, at 1505 NE Pioneer Rd.

N) SAND-LO MOTEL/TRAILER PARK
15 campsites w/full hookups, plus 4 tent sites - no fire pits, reservations (800) 676-2601, showers, laundry, restaurant, groceries, fish cleaning area, $12 to $16/night.

North of Long Beach 1 mile, right on State Hwy. 103.

O) MA & PA'S PACIFIC RV PARK
50 trailer sites - 44 w/full hookups plus 6 w/water & electricity & grassy tent area, reservations (360) 642-3253, pets okay - $2 fee, showers, laundry, playground, ocean access, $19/night.

North of Long Beach 2 miles on State Hwy. 103.

P) CRANBERRY RV & TRAILER PARK
24 trailer sites w/full hookups, no tents, adults only, reservations (360) 642-2027, showers, rec room, cable tv, $12/night.

Take State Hwy. 103 north of Long Beach 3 miles to Cranberry Road and head east .3 mile.

Q) ANDERSEN'S ON THE OCEAN
74 campsites - 59 w/full hookups plus 15 tent sites, reservations (800) 645-6795, pets okay, group facilities, showers, cable tv, laundry, trailer waste disposal, ocean access, fishing, children's playground, ice, propane, $14 to $18/night.

North of Long Beach 3.5 miles on State Hwy. 103.

R) PEGG'S OCEANSIDE RV PARK
30 campsites w/full hookups, no tents, reservations (360) 642-2451, showers, ocean access, rec room, cable tv, laundry, $14 to $18/night.

Located 4.5 miles north of Long Beach, on State Hwy. 103.

S) EVERGREEN COURT
34 units w/full hookups plus dry camp, tents okay, reservations (360) 665-6351, showers, playground, trailer waste disposal, $10 to $13/night.

North of Long Beach 7.9 miles on State 103, located just north of 22nd Street.

S) OCEAN BAY MOBILE 7 RV PARK
25 campsites - 15 w/full hookups plus 10 tent sites, reservation (360) 665-6933, pets okay, showers, nearby grocery store, $10 to $15/night.

North of Long Beach at 2515 Bay Ave.

T) WESTGATE RV PARK & MOTEL
39 sites w/full hookups - 11 are pull thrus, no tents, reservation information (360) 665-4211, pets okay, showers, rec room, ocean access, fishing, fish cleaning room, $17 to $18/night.

At Klipsan Beach - 7 miles north of Long Beach at 20803 Pacific Highway.

U) OCEAN PARK RESORT
100 units - 80 w/full hookups plus tent area, reservations (360) 665-4585, showers, cable tv, rec room, swimming pool, hot tub, playground, $15/night.

In Ocean Park, .1 mile east of the highway, on 259th Street.

V) OCEAN AIRE TRAILER PARK
46 sites w/full hookups, no tents, trailers to 35', reservations (360) 665-4027, showers, laundry, $15/night.

In Ocean Park, about .1 mile east of the highway, on 260th Street.

Vacation #5

Picturesque Encounters
at the Oregon Coast

This quiet cove along the Oregon Coast, like nearly all of Oregon's coastal beaches, belong to the public, thanks to the foresight of early Oregonians.

FROM THE AUTHOR'S JOURNAL · · ·

Like most Oregonians, I have taken plenty of day trips, weekend excursions, and summer vacations along the beautiful Oregon coast. So many that it is often easier to sort them out by reflecting on the company or activities rather than where they actually took place.

I've enjoyed the fun-filled atmosphere of the northern coast, taken part in the fellowship of coastal artistic communities, been awed by the spectacular beauty of the southern coastline, and spent time in every park along its shores.

But when asked what I like best about the Oregon coast, it can only be one thing. It's not the solitude of an early morning walk along a deserted beach, the cool glow of the sunset as it drops into the Pacific Ocean, or the feeling of community that comes with time spent in one of its many charming towns. Though these are all special, what I like best about the Oregon coast is the romance.

For me, Lincoln City will always be the Oregon coast's most romantic town. It's a town that caters to lovers. John and I were married on one of Lincoln City's beautiful beaches, at high tide, as the sun gently melted into the ocean. No matter how hard you try, it's hard to top that for romance!

Reflections on a lifetime of coastal vacations

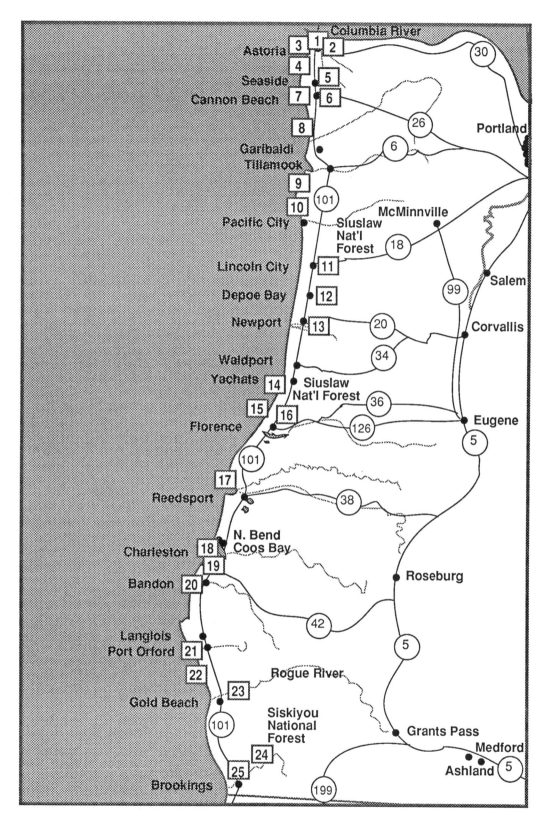

Oregon Coast Attractions

The Oregon coast belongs to everyone. Unlike all of the other coastal states, where most of humanity is restricted to a few overcrowded beaches and wealthy landowners build fences to keep others from invading "their" ocean, nearly all of Oregon's beaches are public. This gives the state 360 miles of spectacular coastal parks.

There are thousands of individual campsites to choose from along the coast, and many more inland a few miles. They include everything from deluxe RV parks with full hookups to quiet natural areas where you can escape the crowds and civilization. In all, this area has more than 200 public campgrounds, and will accommodate up to 11,000 families at one time.

The Oregon coastline varies. Some areas have mountains running right down to the sea, others flat sandy beaches. But best of all, no matter where you go, you'll find plenty of small, secluded beaches. Most are accessible to any visitor willing to hike a bit.

Day-use state and local parks make it easy for the public to enjoy the ocean. They showcase sparkling white sand dunes, agate-strewn beaches, surf-carved caves, forested capes, offshore monoliths, old growth forests, giant rhododendrons, and historic sites.

The North Coast

The northern Oregon coast, with its broad sandy beaches, is where America's west began. Astoria, on the Columbia River, was the first permanent U.S. settlement this side of the Rocky Mountains.

Some of Astoria's early buildings still stand, including **Flavel House [1]**. This elegant 1883 Victorian-style home was built by a local sea captain. For a small fee you can tour the house between 11:00 a.m. and 4:00 p.m. Flavel House is at 8th and Duane Streets.

Astoria's **Columbia River Maritime Museum [2]** showcases 200 years of nautical history. You'll find lots of ship models, naval displays, and nautical artifacts inside. Outside, you can tour the west coast's last seagoing lighthouse, the lightship Columbia. Located on the waterfront, at 17th Street, and open daily from 9:30 a.m. to 5:00 p.m., the charge is minimal.

Fort Stevens [3] was an important military base from 1865 to 1947. Today it is a state park. You can tour the fort's old buildings and batteries year round, and in the summer they put on living history skits. The buildings are open daily from 10:00 a.m. to 6:00 p.m. in the summer; the rest of the year they are only open Wednesday thru Sunday and close at 4:00 p.m.

At **Fort Clatsop [4]**, 5 miles south of Astoria, you can tour a replica of Lewis and Clark's 1805 winter encampment for a $2 fee. Open year round, from 8:00 a.m. to 5:00 p.m., the old fort has been recreated and exhibits explain the significance of this historic journey.

The north coast is full of interesting little resort towns, and a good family destination. The town of **Seaside [5]** sports a fun-filled promenade and is a favorite with teenage visitors. **Cannon Beach [6]** is a charming artistic community popular with Northwest residents.

Photo Courtesy of The Friends of old Ft. Stevens

Civil War re-enactments are held at Fort Stevens throughout the summer, providing a great way for children to learn history while having a good time.

At **Ecola State Park [7]** you'll find a setting that was described by Lewis and Clark as *"the grandest and most pleasing prospect which my eyes have ever surveyed."* **Oswald West State Park [8]** protects a rain forest of massive spruce and cedar. Other outstanding nearby state park attractions include **Cape Meares' Octopus Tree [9]**, and **Cape Kiwanda's tidepools [10]**.

The Central Coast

The central Oregon coast is also popular with vacationers. Defined as the land that lies between Cascade Head and Coos Bay, it too has lots of great family vacation spots.

The skies over **Lincoln City [11]** are nearly always filled with kites. Beachcombers, waterskiers, windsurfers and anglers are drawn to its seashore; shoppers like the factory outlet mall and its quaint little shops.

Depoe Bay's **Devil's Churn [12]** is a wonderful natural attraction. At high tide this saltwater geyser spouts 60 feet into the air. Gray whales are also commonly spotted offshore here between December and May.

Newport [13] is where you'll find the wonderful new Oregon Coast Aquarium, Hatfield Marine Science Center, Ripley's

The Oregon Dunes extend from Florence to Coos Bay. They present a gorgeous view, and are one of the largest coastal sand dune areas in the world.

Believe It or Not Museum, an under-sea garden, and a wax museum. All are great family attractions, but if you don't have time to tour them all, you should at least allow time for the new aquarium, it houses the captive whale made famous by the film Free Willy.

The outdoor exhibits at the Oregon Coast Aquarium also provide an opportunity to see seals, sea otters and puffin in near-natural surroundings. Indoors you'll find a beautifully lighted jellyfish tank, lots of hands-on exhibits, a great film on whales, and a whole lot more. The aquarium is open every day but Christmas, from 9:00 a.m. to 6:00 p.m., and the charge is $3.50 to $7.75, depending on your age.

Cape Perpetua [14], just south of Yachats, is a great place to learn what this area was like 40 million years ago. At the visitors' center you'll discover how the land evolved, see artifacts left behind by early Native Americans, retrace the region's discovery by non-natives, and inspect Indian shell midden. Interpretive trails and nature walks make this a fun place to visit.

The world famous **Sea Lion Caves [15]**, 10 miles south of the cape, is where you'll find a colony of Steller sea lions occupying America's largest sea cave. Visitors take an elevator down into the cave to where they can safely watch the one-ton mammals in their open-sea environment. Open year round, from

9:00 a.m. to just before dusk, the cost is $3.50 to $5.50.

Darlingtonia State Park [16], 5 miles north of Florence, has raised wooden walkways that allow you to stroll through a sea of unusual carnivorous plants.

The **Oregon Dunes National Recreation Area [17]** extends from Florence to Coos Bay. This 40-mile stretch is one of the largest coastal dune areas in the world. A number of parks line the area, making it a great vacation destination. You'll find miles of sparkling white sand dunes, great beaches for walking or sunbathing, protected wildlife areas, and lots of good hiking trails.

Dune buggy enthusiasts rank the Oregon Dunes among the West's most challenging. Even if you're not a participant, the buggies are fun to watch.

The South Coast

Oregon's south coast is where you'll find those forested mountains that begin right at the water's edge. Miles of unoccupied shoreland exist between the scattered towns, providing endless views of the ocean.

Shore Acres State Park saw its beginnings as a private estate. Its beautiful maintained floral gardens and picturesque views make it a great place to spend a sunny afternoon.

Shore Acres State Park [18], west of Coos Bay, is best known for its beautiful turn-of-the-century floral gardens. These gardens are all that's left of a beautiful old estate that once stood here.

Attractions include a lovely Japanese garden, 100-foot lily pond, and a spectacular collection of plants that were brought by sailing ships from all over the world. Outside the gardens, the sea pounds relentlessly against the sheer cliffs, creating a beautiful sculpted landscape.

Charleston is a popular charter fishing destination, and also where you'll find the **South Slough Estuary [19]**. Located four miles south of town, on Seven Devils Road, the estuary's trails and waterways can be enjoyed year round. During the summer, the interpretive center is open from 8:30 a.m. to 4:30 p.m. For a schedule of activities call (541) 888-5558.

Bandon [20] is a great spot for whale watching, and **Port Orford [21]** beaches are generally uncrowded. **Humbug Mountain State Park [22]**, 6 miles south of Port Orford, has a trail leading to the mountain's top that provides spectacular views of the coastline.

Gold Beach sits at the mouth of the **Rogue River [23]**. Designated a wild and scenic river, 84 miles of its pristine beauty are protected from further development. From the mouth of the Applegate River to Lobster Creek, you

Beaches in Southern Oregon are often empty, making them great for those seeking solitude.

can see the river only by boat or on foot. Tours operate on the lower part of the river, offering visitors a thrilling wild river experience.

Loeb State Park [24], 10 miles east of Brookings, is situated along the Chetco River. This 320-acre setting is a wonderful place to spend the day, wandering thru large groves of myrtlewood and redwood trees. The redwood grove is the most northerly in the U.S.

Brookings is in Oregon's banana belt, so the temperature there is generally warmer than the rest of the coast. If you visit between April and July, stop at **Azalea State Park [25]** where you'll find 300-year-old azaleas in bloom. The colors are brilliant, making this a lovely spot for hiking or a romantic picnic.

Between mid-May and the end of September, a $3.00 per day vehicle fee is charged at some of the most popular state parks. Seasonal permits are $20.00. If you camp in a state park, your receipt also serves as a day-use permit on the same day(s) you are registered for overnight camping.

The Oregon coast is a picture-perfect place for a family camping vacation. Whether you choose just one destination for your entire vacation, or spend your time wandering up and down the coastline, you're in for an unparalleled coastal experience.

For Additional Information

Visitor information centers are a great source for details on local attractions and activities. Call 3-4 weeks before your trip and you'll receive lots of brochures, maps, and other useful information.

Visitor information centers:

Astoria
(503) 325-6311
Bandon
(541) 347-9616
Brookings Area
(800) 535-9469
Cannon Beach
(503) 436-2623
Coos Bay Area
(800) 824-8486
Depoe Bay
(541) 765-2889
Florence
(541) 997-3128
Gold Beach
(800) 525-2334
Lincoln City
(800) 452-2151
Newport
(800) 262-7844
Port Orford
(541) 332-8055
Seaside
(888) 306-2326
Tillamook
(503) 842-7525
Waldport
(541) 563-2133

Oregon Coast Accommodations
(Towns listed north to south)

ASTORIA

Astoria Dunes Motel (800) 441-3319
288 W Marine Dr. (503) 325-7111
58 rooms, handicap access, river view,
indoor pool & spa, laundry, $38-75.

Bayshore Motor Inn (800) 621-0641
555 Hamburg Ave. (503) 325-2205
77 rooms, handicap access, kitchen
units, indoor pool, jacuzzi, sauna,
laundry, pets okay, river view, $55-85,
includes continental breakfast.

Franklin Street B&B (800) 448-1098
1140 Franklin (503) 325-4314
5 rooms/suites w/private baths in
handsome antique-furnished Victorian
home, kids okay, $68-120.

Red Lion Inn (800) 547-8010
400 Industry St. (503) 325-7373
124 rooms, kitchen units, handicap
access, pets okay, restaurant/lounge,
river view, $85-95.

Rivershore Motel (800) 253-2921
59 W Marine Dr. (503) 325-2921
43 rooms, handicap access, kitchen
units, river view, $40-68.

Rosebriar Hotel B&B (800) 487-0224
636 14th St. (503) 325-7427
11 rooms in elegantly restored former
convent, private baths, kitchens, fire
places, handicap access, spa, river
view, $59-139, inc. gourmet breakfast.

SEASIDE

Best Western Ocean View Resort
(800) 234-8439 or (503) 738-3334
414 N Prom
104 rooms, some w/kitchens, fireplace, in-room jacuzzi, ocean view,
handicap access, indoor pool & spa,
rest./lounge, $65-265.

Comfort Inn Boardwalk
(800) 228-5150 or (503) 738-3011
545 Broadway
65 rooms, handicap access, kitchens,
pets okay, fireplaces, $65-175.

Ebb-Tide Motel (800) 468-6232
300 N Prom (503) 738-8371
99 rooms, ocean view, kitchens, fireplace & in-room jacuzzi units, handicap access, indoor pool & spa, no pets,
$80-180 ($60-105).

Edgewater Inn at the Prom
(800) 822-3170 or (503) 738-4142
341 S Prom
14 rooms, handicap access, pets okay,
kitchens, fireplace & in-room jacuzzi
units, ocean view, $69-159.

Sand & Sea Condos (800) 628-2371
475 S Prom (503) 738-8441
28 luxury 1-2 bedroom condos on
beach, handicap access, fireplaces,
indoor pool & sauna, $85-246.

Shilo Inn Oceanfront (800) 222-2244
30 N Prom (503) 738-9571
112 rooms, ocean view, kitchen & fireplace units, handicap access, indoor
pool, jacuzzi, exercise room, restau-
rant/lounge, $79-220.

CANNON BEACH

Cannon Beach Hotel Lodgings
1116 S Hemlock (503) 436-1392
26 rooms in three inns @ entrance to
Haystack Rock, no pets or smoking,
$49-149.

Hallmark Resort (800) 345-5676
1400 S Hemlock (503) 436-1566
132 family suites w/kitchenettes -
many w/in-room spas & fireplaces,
indoor pool, exercise center, pets welcome w/prior approval, $89-145.

McBee Motel Cottages
888 S Hemlock (503) 436-2569
12 rooms, no smoking, pets welcome,
$39-135.

Stephanie Inn (800) 633-3466
2740 S Pacific St. (503) 446-2221
46 units w/fireplaces & in-room spas,
view of Haystack Rock, no smoking, no
pets, no kids under 12, dining room,
$109-199, includes breakfast buffet.

Surfsand Resort (800) 547-6100
Oceanfront & Gower (503) 436-2274
88 units, fireplace, ocean view, indoor
pool & jacuzzi, laundry, $109-229.

Tolovana Inn (800) 333-8890
3400 S Hemlock (503) 436-2311
178 units - some w/kitchen, fireplace
& spa, ocean view, pool, $68-239.

TILLAMOOK

Mar Clair Inn (800) 331-6857
11 Main Ave. (503) 842-7571
47 units - 6 w/kitchenettes, pets okay
w/credit card - $6 fee, pool, $42-99.

Shilo Inn (800) 222-2244
2515 US Hwy 101 N (503) 842-7971
100 units - 6 w/kitchenettes, pool,
river view, pets okay - $7 fee, $59-115.

Tillamook Inn (503) 842-4413
1810 US Hwy. 101 N
27 units, 1 kitchen unit, $38-90.

Western Royal Inn (800) 624-2912
1125 N Main Ave. (503) 842-8844
40 units, small pets okay - $5 fee,
pool, $45-95.

LINCOLN CITY

Coho Inn (800) 848-7006
1635 NW Harbor (541) 994-3684
50 units, many w/fireplace & ocean
view, pets okay - fee, indoor jacuzzi &
sauna, handicap access, $58-80.

Ester Lee Motel (888) 996-3606
3803 SW US Hwy. 101 (541) 996-3606
53 ocean view rooms - many w/fire-
place & kitchen, small pets okay,
handicap access, $54-74.

Inn at Spanish Head (800) 452-8127
4009 SW US Hwy. 101 (541) 996-2161
120 ocean view condos, kitchens,
sauna, pool, exercise room, laundry,
10th floor rest./lounge, $102-179.

Sea Gypsy (800) 452-6929
145 NW Inlet (541) 994-5266
136 units - some w/kit., indoor pool,
no pets, handicap access, $55-110.

Sea Horse Oceanfront Lodging
(800) 662-2101 or (541) 994-2101
2039 NW Harbor
55 units - some w/fireplace, indoor
pool, spa, some pets, $45-125.

Shilo Inn Resort (800) 222-2244
1501 NW 40th Place (541) 994-3655
247 oceanfront units w/microwave &
ref., many w/fireplace, indoor pool,
sauna, exercise room, jacuzzi, laundry,
handicap access, $54-175.

DEPOE BAY AREA

Gracie's Landing B&B Inn
(800) 228-0448 or (541) 765-2322
235 SE Bay View Ave - Depoe Bay
13 spacious harbor view rooms - some
w/fireplace & spa, handicap access,
$80-105, includes gourmet breakfast.

Inn at Otter Crest
(800) 452-2101 or (541) 765-2111
Located in Otter Rock - south of DB
102 units - many w/fireplace & kit.,
oceanfront, some w/in-room jacuzzi,
pool, hot tub, rest./lounge, $90-149.

Salishan Lodge (800) 452-2300
In Gleneden Beach (541) 764-3600
205 units - many w/fireplace, view of
bay, handicap access, pool, jacuzzi,
sauna, rest./lounge, tennis, 18-hole
golf course, pets okay, $110-210.

NEWPORT

Agate Beach Motel (800) 755-5674
175 NW Gilbert Way (541) 265-8746
10 units, secluded, kitchens, oceanfront, pets okay, $115 ($85).

Hotel Newport @ Agate Beach
(800) 547-3310
3019 N Coast Hwy.
146 units, overlooks ocean & lighthouse, pool, jacuzzi, pets okay, handicap access, rest./pub, $104-155.

Shilo Inn Oceanfront Resort
536 SW Elizabeth (800) 222-2244
179 rooms - some w/fireplace, pool,
spa, restaurant, sports bar, some pets
okay, $105-155.

Sylvia Beach Hotel (541) 265-5428
267 NW Cliff St.
20 rooms in 1910 oceanfront B&B,
book lovers delight, handicap access,
no smoking, restaurant, $60-139.

Val-U Inn Motel (800) 443-7777
531 SW Fall St.
71 rooms/suites, in-room jacuzzis,
near beach, laundry, handicap access,
$48-98, inc. deluxe cont. breakfast.

Viking's Cottages (800) 480-2477
729 NW Coast St. (541) 265-2477
14 Cape Cod cottages w/fp & kit.,
oceanfront, pets okay, $65-80.

WALDPORT/YACHATS

Adobe Resort Motel
(800) 522-3623 or (541) 547-3141
1555 US Hwy. 101 - Yachats
96 units - some w/kit. & FP, ocean
view, pets okay, sauna, rest., $55-200.

Bayshore Inn (541) 563-3202
902 NW Bayshore Dr. - Waldport
92 units, bay view, pool & jacuzzi,
restaurant, small pets okay, $40-160.

Deane's Oceanside Lodge
7365 US Hwy 101 - South of Waldport
17 units - 2 w/kitchens, ocean view,
$58-85.

Fireside Resort Motel
(800) 336-3573 or (541) 547-3636
1881 US Hwy. 101 - Yachats
43 rooms - some w/jacuzzi & fireplace
plus 3 vacation houses, ocean view -
great for storm watching, refrigerators,
pets okay, $47-125.

Waldport Motel (541) 563-3035
Downtown Waldport
13 units - some w/kitchens, small
pets okay, $30-65

FLORENCE

Best Western Pier Point Inn
(800) 435-6736 or (541) 997-7191
85625 US Hwy. 101 S
55 rooms, sauna, wheelchair access,
$59-89, inc. continental breakfast.

Blue Heron Inn B&B (800) 997-7780
6563 State Hwy 126 (541) 997-4091
6 rooms w/private bath, spectacular
view of Siuslaw River, no pets $65-100
($55-90), includes gourmet breakfast.

Driftwood Shores (800) 422-5091
88416 First Ave. (541) 997-8263
136 rooms, on beach, kitchens, indoor
pool, wheelchair access, rest./lounge,
$73-245.

Holiday Inn Express (800) HOLIDAY
2475 US Hwy. 101 (541) 997-7797
51 rooms, hot tub, wheelchair access,
$59-69, inc. continental breakfast.

Park Motel (800) 392-0441
85034 US Hwy. 101 S (541) 997-2634
17 rooms, kitchen avail., pets welcome, picnic area, $39-89.

Silver Sands Motel (541) 997-3459
1449 US Hwy. 101
50 rooms, kitchens, pool, pets okay,
$38-58.

COOS BAY/CHARLESTON

Best Western Holiday Motel
(800) 228-8655 or (541) 269-5111
411 N Bayshore - CB
77 units - some w/kitchen & jacuzzi,
indoor pool, sauna, pets okay, wheelchair access, laundry, rest., $59-125.

Captain John's Motel (541) 888-4041
8061 Kingfisher Dr. - Charleston
46 units, kitchen & jacuzzi units,
wheelchair access, $40-70.

Coos Bay Manor B&B (800) 269-1224
955 S 5th St. (541) 269-1224
5 bedrooms - 3 w/private bath in
majestic 1912 Colonial-style home,
$75-100, inc. full breakfast.

Edgewater Inn (800) 233-0423
275 E Johnson - CB (541) 267-0423
81 units, kitchen & jacuzzi units, pool,
spa, sauna, fitness room, pets okay,
wheelchair access, $65-70.

Plainview Motel (541) 888-5166
2760 Cape Arago Hwy. - Charleston
10 units, kitchens, pets okay, $34-50.

Red Lion Inn (800) 733-5466
1313 N Bayshore - CB (541) 267-4141
143 rooms, pool, rest./lounge, wheelchair access, pets okay, $69-104.

Timber Lodge Motel (800) 782-7592
1001 N Bayshore - CB (541) 267-7066
53 rooms, jacuzzi units, wheelchair
access, pets okay, rest., $29-40.

BANDON

Harbor View Motel
(800) 526-0209 or (541) 347-4417
US Hwy. 101 in Old Town
59 units, handicap access, jacuzzi,
walk to rest. & galleries, $74-82.

Inn @ Face Rock (800) 638-3092
3225 Beach Loop Rd. (541) 347-9441
55 units - suites w/kit. & fireplace,
beach access, near rest. & golf course,
$49-129, inc. cont. breakfast.

Lighthouse B&B (541) 347-9316
650 Jetty Road
5 rooms w/jacuzzis & fireplaces, ocean
& river views, inc. full breakfast, no
pets or kids under 12, $90-145.

Sea Star AYH Hostel (541) 347-9632
375 Second St.
3 small carpeted dorms & 3 family
rooms, fully-equipped kitchen, common room, showers, all ages, $12-26.

Sunset Motel (800) 842-2407
1755 Beach Loop Rd. (541) 347-2453
57 units, kit. & fireplace units, ocean
view, spa, rest./lounge, $53-175.

Table Rock Motel (541) 347-2700
840 Beach Loop Rd.
15 units - 5 w/kitchens, ocean view &
beach access, pets okay, $30-90.

GOLD BEACH

Gold Beach Resort (800) 541-0947
29232 Hwy. 101 (541) 247-7066
40 units, kitchens, ocean view, pool,
spa, handicap access, no pets, $89-99.

Inn @ Gold Beach (800) 503-0833
1435 Ellensburg (541) 247-6606

41 units - some w/kitchen, ocean
view, pets okay, $35-125.

Ireland's Rustic Lodges
1120 S Ellensburg (541) 247-7718
40 cottages/cabins - some w/kitchen
& fireplace, ocean view, pool, spa,
sauna, exercise room, laundry, handicap access, pets okay, $47-61.

River Bridge Inn (800) 759-4533
1010 Jerry's Flat Rd. (541) 247-4533
50 units, view of Rogue River, $45-85.

Shore Cliff Inn by the Sea
1100 Ellensburg (541) 247-7091
38 units, ocean view, handicap access,
$55-75.

Western Village Motel (541) 247-6611
975 S. Ellensburg Ave.
27 units, kitchen & fireplace units,
ocean view, pets okay, $30-50.

BROOKINGS

Beaver State (541) 469-5361
437 Chetco Avenue
17 rooms, kitchenettes, pets okay,
downtown, $39-55.

Chetco River Inn (800) 327-2688
21202 High Prairie Rd. (541) 670-1645
4 rooms w/private bath, no smoking,
on Chetco River, $115-135 (85-95),
inc. gourmet breakfast.

Holmes Sea Cove (541) 469-3025
17350 Holmes Dr.
3 rooms w/microwave & ref., no smoking, oceanfront, $80-95, includes cont.
breakfast in room.

South Coast Inn B&B
(800) 525-9273 or (541) 469-5557
516 Redwood St.
4 rooms in spacious 1917 home plus
garden cottage w/kitchen, no smoking,
no pets, no kids under 12, spa,
jacuzzi, downtown, ocean view, $79-
89, includes full breakfast.

Spindrift Motor Inn (800) 292-1171
1215 Chetco Avenue (541) 469-5345
35 rooms, kitchenettes, downtown,
ocean view, $45-59.

Oregon Coast Campgrounds & RV Parks

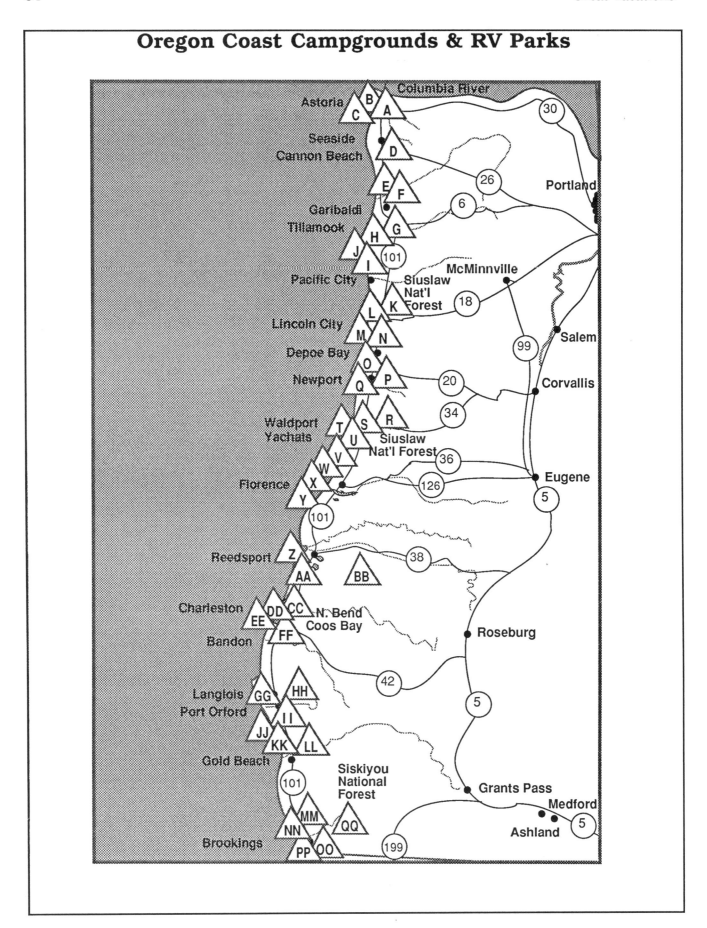

A) ASTORIA KOA

310 units, 142 w/full hookups, 87 w/water & elec., tent sites & cabins, reservations (800) KOA-8506, handicap access, fire rings, showers, laundry, store, indoor pool, playground, bicycle rentals, pets okay, $22 to $41/night.

West of Astoria 10 miles, across from Fort Stevens State Park.

B) FORT STEVENS STATE PARK

605 units, 213 w/full hookups, 128 w/elec., 253 tent units, 5 group areas & 9 yurts, reservations (800) 551-6949 or (503) 861-1671, maximum site 69', wheelchair access, picnic area, showers, trailer waste disposal, boat launch, fishing, ocean access, bicycle & hiking trails, $11 to $20/night - yurts $27.

West of Astoria 10 miles, near Warrenton.

C) KAMPERS WEST KAMPGROUND RV PARK

250 units, 137 w/full hookups, 50 w/water & electricity, plus tent sites, reservations (800) 880-5267, showers, laundry, trailer waste disposal, river, fishing, pets okay, $15 to $20/night.

West of Astoria 10 miles at 1140 NW Warrenton. Follow Fort Stevens signs.

D) RV RESORT AT CANNON BEACH

100 trailer sites w/full hookups, no tents, reservations (503) 436-2231, showers, laundry, cable tv, groceries, swimming pool, therapy pool, river, fishing, game room, playfield, playground, hiking, wheelchair access, $33 to $55/night.

At Cannon Beach – just off the Cannon Beach exit ramp; about .6 mile past milepost 29.

E) NEHALEM BAY STATE PARK

284 campsites w/elec., 17 site horse camp w/corrals, plus 9 yurts, maximum site 60', wheelchair access, reservations (800) 551-6949 or (503) 368-5154, picnic area, showers, trailer waste disposal, boat launch, fishing, ocean access, bicycle trail, horse trails, $14 to $19/night - yurts $27.

South of Cannon Beach 17 miles; park is 3 miles past Manzanita Jct. on 101.

F) BAR VIEW JETTY COUNTY PARK

260 campsites, 60 w/full hookups, plus 200 tent units, reservations (503) 322-3477, showers, trailer waste disposal, ocean access/swimming, fishing, playground, hiking, pets okay, $14 to $18/night.

North of Garibaldi 2 miles on US 101.

G) PLEASANT VALLEY RV PARK

85 campsites, 15 w/full hookups, 60 w/water & elec., plus 10 tent sites, reservations (503) 842-4779, showers, laundry, groceries, playground, cable tv, trailer waste disposal, river, fishing, hiking, propane, pets okay, $14 to $20/night.

South of Tillamook 6 miles on US 101.

H) CAPE LOOKOUT STATE PARK

250 units, 53 w/full hookups, 197 tent sites, group tent areas & 4 yurts, maximum site 60', reservations (800) 551-6949 or (503) 842-4981, picnic area, wheelchair access, showers, trailer waste disposal, hiking, ocean beach, fishing, $16 to $20/night - yurts $27 - group sites $60.

Southwest of Tillamook. Leave US 101 at Tillamook and head southwest 12 miles to campground.

I) CAPE KIWANDA RV PARK

158 campsites, 109 w/full hookups, 19 w/water & elec., plus 30 tent sites, reservations (503) 965-6230, showers, laundry, cable tv, groceries, trailer waste disposal, swimming, fishing, pets okay, $15 to $21/night.

North of Pacific City. At city center take Brooten Road west .2 mile, then head north 1 mile to campground.

J) SAND BEACH NF CAMP

101 units, trailers to 32', flush toilets, trailer waste disposal, ORV area – dunes, boating, fishing, in Siuslaw NF, $12/night.

North of Pacific City 6 miles. CR 536 west .2 mile, CR 535 north 8.4 miles, CR 503 west 1 mile to camp road.

K) LINCOLN CITY KOA

85 campsites, 23 w/full hookups, 29 w/water & elec., plus 32 tent units &

10 cabins, reservations (541) 994-2961, showers, laundry, groceries, game room, propane, trailer waste disposal, playground, pets okay, $19 to $24/night - cabins $35.

Northeast of Lincoln City. Take US 101 north 4 miles, East Devils Lake Road southeast 1 mile.

L) DEVIL'S LAKE STATE PARK

100 units - 32 w/full hookups plus 68 tent sites, reservations (800) 452-5867 or (541) 994-2002, maximum site 62', wheelchair access, showers, boat launch, on East Devil's Lake, boating, fishing, swimming, $13 to $20/night.

In Lincoln City, just off US 101.

M) SEA & SAND RV PARK

95 campsites w/full hookups, no tents, trailers to 35', reservation information - (541) 764-2313, wheelchair access, showers, laundry, trailer waste disposal, swimming, fishing, $21/night.

Located north of Depoe Bay 3.5 miles on US 101.

N) FOGARTY CREEK RV PARK

53 trailer sites w/full hookups - no tents allowed, reservations (541) 764-2228, showers, cable tv, laundry, trailer waste disposal, $21/night.

Located north of Depoe Bay 2 miles on US 101.

O) BEVERLY BEACH STATE PARK

279 sites, 53 w/full hookups, 76 w/elec., 136 tent units, hiker/biker camp, plus 14 yurts, reservations (800) 452-5687 or (541) 265-9278, maximum site 65', picnic area, wheelchair access, showers, trailer waste disposal, ocean access, hiking, $4 to $20/night & $27 for yurt.

Located north of Newport 7 miles on US 101.

P) HARBOR VILLAGE TRAILER PARK

140 trailer sites w/full hookups, no tents, information (541) 265-5088, showers, laundry, $15/night.

Go east of Newport .5 mile on US 20, take SW Moore Drive south .5 mile, and SE Bay Blvd. east 1 block.

Q) SOUTH BEACH STATE PARK

244 sites w/elec., hiker/biker camp, 3 group tent areas & 10 yurts, reservations (800) 551-6949 or (541) 867-4715, maximum site 60', wheelchair access, showers, trailer waste disposal, ocean access, $4 to $20/night - group area $60 & $27 for a yurt.

South of Newport 2 miles on US 101.

R) DRIFT CREEK LANDING

60 trailer sites - 52 w/full hookups, plus 8 w/water & electricity, no tents, information (541) 563-3610, showers, laundry, river, fishing, boat launch & rental, pets okay, $18 to $20/night.

East of Waldport 3.7 miles on State Hwy. 34.

S) BEACHSIDE STATE PARK

82 units - 32 w/hookups for elec., plus 50 tent sites & hiker/biker camp, reservations (800) 551-6949 or (541) 563-3220, maximum site 30', picnic area, showers, ocean access, $4 to $20/night.

South of Waldport 4 miles on US 101.

T) TILLICUM BEACH NF CAMP

57 units, trailers to 32', piped water, flush toilets, ocean view campsites, fishing, in Siuslaw NF, pets okay, $12/night.

South of Waldport 4.7 miles on US 101.

U) CAPE PERPETUA NF CAMP

37 units, group site, information (541) 563-3211, trailers to 22', stream, flush toilets, trailer waste disposal, interpretive serv., fishing, hiking, ocean access, in Siuslaw NF, pets okay, $12/night.

South of Yachats 2.7 miles on US 101.

V) SEA PERCH RV PARK & CAMP

48 units - 21 w/full hookups, 27 w/water & electricity, plus 4 tent sites, reservations - (541) 547-3505, showers, laundry, ocean access, swimming, fishing, pets okay, $19 to $23/night.

South of Yachats 6.5 miles on US 101.

W) SUTTON NF CAMPGROUND

90 units, trailers to 22' - no hookups, flush toilets, fishing, trail to ocean, in Siuslaw NF, $12/night.

Go north of Florence 6 miles on US 101, then take FSR 794 northwest 1.6 miles.

X) JESSIE M. HONEYMAN STATE PARK

378 campsites, 50 w/full hookups, 91 w/elec., 237 tent sites, hiker/biker camp, 6 group tent areas & 4 yurts, reservations (800) 551-6949 or (541) 888-4902, maximum site 55', picnic area, wheelchair access, showers, trailer waste disposal, boat launch, fishing, swimming, hiking trails, sand dunes, lakes, $4 to $20/night - group area $60 & yurts $27.

South of Florence 3 miles on US 101.

Y) DRIFTWOOD II FS CAMP

70 units, trailers to 50', no hookups, piped water, flush toilets – wheelchair access, ocean fishing, hiking, ORV, in Siuslaw NF, pets okay, $13/night.

South of Florence 7 miles via US 101, FSR 1078 west 1.4 miles.

Z) SURFWOOD CAMPGROUND

163 campsites, 100 w/full hookups, 41 w/water & electricity, plus 22 tent units, reservations (541) 271-4020, showers, laundry, groceries, swimming pool, playground, tennis, trailer waste disposal, stream, pets okay, $12 to $16/night.

Southwest of Reedsport 2 miles on US 101.

AA) WILLIAM M. TUGMAN STATE PARK

115 campsites w/electricity, maximum site to 50', reservations (800) 551-6949 or (541) 888-4902, wheelchair access, showers, trailer waste disposal, boat launch, fishing, swimming, $15/night.

South of Reedsport 8 miles on US 101.

BB) LOON LAKE LODGE RESORT

100 campsites, 37 w/water & electricity, plus 78 w/no hookups, tents okay, reservations (541) 599-2244, groceries, restaurant/lounge, lake, swimming, fishing, boat launch, boat rental, hiking, pets okay, $15 to $18/night.

Southeast of Reedsport. State 38 east 13 miles, then CR 3 south 8.2 miles.

CC) CHARLESTON MARINA & RV PARK

110 units w/full hookups plus tent sites, trailers to 45', reservations (541) 888-9512, showers, laundry, trailer waste disposal, ocean access, river, fishing, boat launch, playground, pets okay, $14/night.

At west end of Charleston Bridge head north on Boat Basin Drive for 2 blocks and turn east on Kingfisher Drive.

DD) BASTENDORFF BEACH COUNTY PARK

81 units - 56 w/water & elec., plus 25 tent sites, trailers to 45', information (541) 888-5353, wheelchair access, showers, trailer waste disposal, flush toilets, playground, ocean access, fishing, pets okay, $8 to $12/night.

South of Charleston 2 miles via the Cape Arago Highway.

EE) SUNSET BAY STATE PARK

139 campsites - 29 w/hookups plus 34 w/elec., 72 tent units, 11 group tent areas, hiker/biker camp & 4 yurts, maximum 47', reservations (800) 551-6949 or (541) 888-4902, picnic area, wheelchair access, showers, beach access, $4 to $19/night - group area $60 & yurts $27.

South of Charleston, on Sunset Bay.

FF) BULLARDS BEACH STATE PARK

192 sites - 92 w/full hookups, 99 w/elec., hiker/biker camp, 6 yurts & 8 site horse camp w/4 double corrals, maximum site 55', reservations (800) 551-6949 or (541) 347-2209, wheelchair access, showers, trailer waste disp., boat launch, fishing, horse trails, $4 to $19/night - yurts $27.

North of Bandon 1 mile on US 101.

GG) BANDON/PORT ORFORD KOA

74 campsites - 16 w/full hookups, 24 w/water & elec., plus 34 tent units & 6 cabins, reservations (541) 348-2358, showers, laundry, trailer waste disposal, playground, hiking, pets okay, $17 to $22/night - cabins $32.

South of Langlois about 3 miles on US 101.

HH) CAPE BLANCO STATE PARK

58 campsites w/hookups for elec., hiker/biker camp, 4 group tent areas & 6 site horse camp w/3 double corrals, maximum site 65', reservations (800) 551-6949 or (541) 332-6774, wheelchair access, showers, trailer waste disposal, fishing, ocean access, black sand beach, hiking, $4 to $18/night - group area $60.

Head northwest of Port Orford for 4 miles on US 101, then follow signs west 5 miles.

II) HUMBUG MOUNTAIN STATE PARK

108 campsites, 30 w/elec., 78 tent units, plus hiker/biker camp, maximum site 55', reservations (800) 551-6949 or (541) 332-6774, picnic area, wheelchair access, showers, trailer waste disposal, ocean access, hiking trail, $4 to $18/night.

Located south of Port Orford 6 miles on US 101.

JJ) ARIZONA BEACH CAMPGROUND

127 campsites, 11 w/full hookups, 85 w/water & electricity, plus 31 tent units, reservations (541) 332-6491, showers, laundry, groceries, trailer waste disposal, swimming, fishing, playfield, pets okay, $18 and up/night.

Located north of Gold Beach 14 miles on US 101.

KK) HONEY BEAR CAMPGROUND

150 campsites, 55 w/full hookups, 18 w/water & electricity, plus 77 tent units, information (541) 247-2765, wheelchair access, showers, laundry, trailer waste disposal, swimming, fishing, playfield, playground, hiking, pets okay, $14 to $17/night.

Go north of Gold Beach 7 miles on US 101, then take Ophir Road north 2 miles to campground.

LL) INDIAN CREEK RECREATION PARK

125 campsites, 100 w/full hookups, plus 25 tent units, reservation information - (541) 247-7704, showers, laundry, river, fishing, playfield, wheelchair access, pets okay, $18 and up/night.

East of Gold Beach. Leave US 101 at south end of Rogue River bridge, and go east .5 mile on Jerry's Flat Road.

MM) HARRIS BEACH STATE PARK

152 units - 34 w/full hookups, 52 w/elec., 66 tent sites, hiker/biker camp & 4 yurts, reservations (800) 551-6949 or (541) 469-2021, maximum site 50', picnic area, wheelchair access, showers, trailer waste disposal, fishing, ocean access, hiking trails, $4 to $19/night - yurts $27.

North of Brookings 2 miles on US 101.

NN) BEACH FRONT RV PARK

184 campsites, 48 w/full hookups, 56 w/water & elec., plus 75 dry sites, tents okay, trailers to 40', reservations (800) 441-0856, showers, laundry, trailer waste disposal, river, swimming, fishing, boat launch, wheelchair access, $9 to $18/night.

In Brookings – take Lower Harbor Road to Benham Lane.

OO) DRIFTWOOD RV PARK

108 units, 100 w/full hookups, plus 8 w/water & elec., no tents, trailers to 70', wheelchair access, reservations (541) 469-3213, showers, laundry, fishing, pets okay, $16 to $20/night.

South of Brookings. US 101 over Chetco River Bridge, to Lower Harbor Road, west .7 mile.

PP) CHETCO RV PARK

120 sites w/full hookups - 80 are pull-thrus, no tents, trailers to 36', adults only, small pets okay, reservations (541) 469-3863, showers, laundry, trailer waste disposal, $17/night.

South of Brookings 1 mile past Chetco River Bridge on US 101.

QQ) LOEB STATE PARK

53 sites w/elec. plus 3 cabins, trailers to 50', reservations - (800) 551-69497 or (541) 469-2021, picnic area, showers, old-growth trees, nature trail, swimming, fishing, rafting, $16/night - cabins $35.

Northeast of Brookings 8 miles on North Bank Road.

Vacation # 6

An Ice Age Vacation In Eastern Washington

Although Lake Roosevelt is popular with anglers, waterskiers and swimmers, it's also large enough to provide plenty of quiet areas for those seeking solitude.

FROM THE AUTHOR'S JOURNAL . . .

There I was, standing at the edge of America's largest waterfall, and without the interpretive center and signs marking its significance I would never have seen it.

Today Dry Falls is just that, dry. But at one time the water rushed over it with enough force to be heard for a hundred miles.

Imagine, a waterfall 3.5 times wider and 2.5 times higher than Niagara Falls. One that appeared almost overnight. Nearly half of North America's glacial floodwaters had thundered through here during the final days of the Ice Age.

This is a trip to be remembered, not for its beauty, although the deserts of eastern Washington can be quite beautiful. This is a trip that will be remembered because it so vividly brings the Ice Age into the present.

After Dry Falls, I viewed the Grand Coulee landscape differently. Those weren't just chasms, valleys and rocks that provided my eyes with a pleasant experience. They were part of a historic time that had, until then, been only a name given to an era I'd had to memorize for a grade school history test.

Notes from my first Ice Age vacation

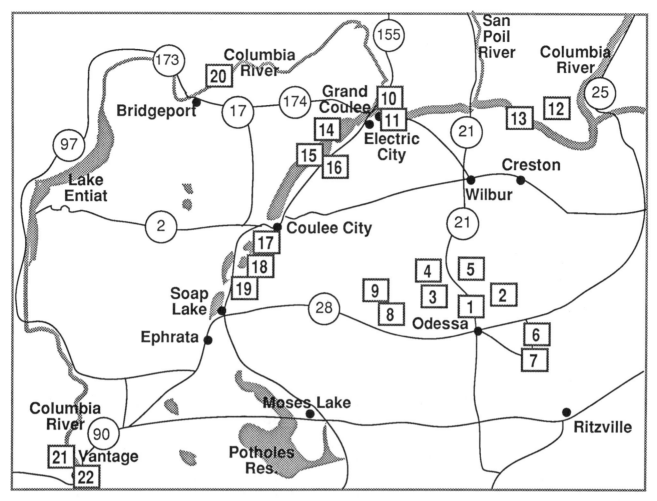

Ice Age Area Attractions

Let your imagination carry you back 13,000 years. You are in eastern Washington, and the gently rolling hills are covered with a 200-foot deep blanket of windblown silt. The 15,000-square-mile area circling current day Odessa is a shallow lava bowl tipped so that its southwest rim is 2,000 feet lower than the northeast edge.

You are witnessing the end of the Ice Age. Massive glaciers have covered the land to the north for more than 750,000 years. They extend southward into the Okanogan, San Poil, Columbia, Colville, and Pend Oreille Valleys. Ice has damned the rivers, creating vast lakes and forcing the water to seek new paths. Glacial Lake Missoula is the largest of all the Ice Age lakes. Its 600 cubic miles of water cover 3,000 square miles of northwest Montana. It is 2000 feet deep near the mammoth ice dam that holds it in the mountains.

Summer arrives and the rain begins to fall. This speeds the melting of winter snow and hastens the retreat of the glaciers' southernmost edges. The added water begins to push Lake Missoula over the top of the dam, and with a thundering crash the dam washes away. The lake empties in less than 48 hours.

As this mammoth wall of water travels, it destroys valley ice dams, adding more water to its volume. Surging into eastern Washington's giant lava bowl, it picks up speed at an alarming rate.

The land is scraped bare, and giant slabs of rock are pulled from the earth. The rivers are 20 miles wide, up to 600 feet deep, and move at 45 miles per hour. Within two weeks, most of the water makes its way to the sea, leaving behind a drastically altered landscape.

Thousands of years later you can still see the course taken by that massive wall of water. Giant ripple marks, large deposits of foreign rocks and boulders, huge gravel bars, formidable river deltas, and isolated dry islands forever mark its path. The rolling hills have been replaced by abrupt rock cliffs, oddly carved canyons, giant cataracts, and 200-foot-deep plunge pools.

Eastern Washington has long caught the interest of vacationers. They come to play in the waters of the Columbia, Snake and Spokane Rivers, most never knowing how this strange landscape was created.

Someday, visitors will come just to view the channeled scablands carved by that destructive rush of water we now call the Spokane Flood. Today's visitors can enjoy it naturally, before signs mark every feature and souvenir shops dot the horizon.

Seeing the Ice Age Features
The **Odessa Visitor Center [1]** is a good place to start your Ice Age vacation. You can watch a short video showing how the scablands were formed and pick up a free driving tour brochure. The brochure will help you find a number of close-in places where the flood's devastation is still visible.

Odessa is right in the center of the great flood's middle channel, on the **Crab Creek Floodway [2]**. This region is like no other part of Washington. It consists of a hodge-podge collection of dry canyons and water-ravaged craters.

This land was once covered with great seas of lava. They came in floods, each covering the last, which gives the surrounding cliffs a variety of textures. Look closely, and you can easily see where the different flows of red hot lava begin and end.

Take Lakeview Ranch Road three miles north of town, and you'll find 5,000 acres of Ice Age landscape to explore. This is **Lakeview Ranch [3]**, a rugged BLM property that also offers primitive campsites, pit toilets, drinking water, picnic tables, shade, horse and hiking trails, a horse-loading chute and corrals.

Lakeview Ranch is a good home base for campers who plan to do extensive scabland exploration. Special ranch features include the serene Lake Creek Coulee, enormous Lakeview Ranch Crater, a maze of anastomosing channels, Waukesha Spring, and lots of desert rangeland.

There's also a wonderful collection of flood-ravaged volcano craters seven miles north of Odessa, at the junction of Highway 21 and Coffeepot Road. **Cache**

Crater [4] is west of the highway; **Rock Rose, Hidden Crater, Wild Garden, Amphitheater and Cinnamon Roll [5]** are all to the east. Each crater is different, but all show the effects of the flood on the ancient lava. Trails allow for close-up exploration, but keep your eyes peeled for rattlesnakes and porcupines.

You'll find additional Ice Age features by heading east of Odessa 13 miles on State Highway 28 to Lamona Road. This road

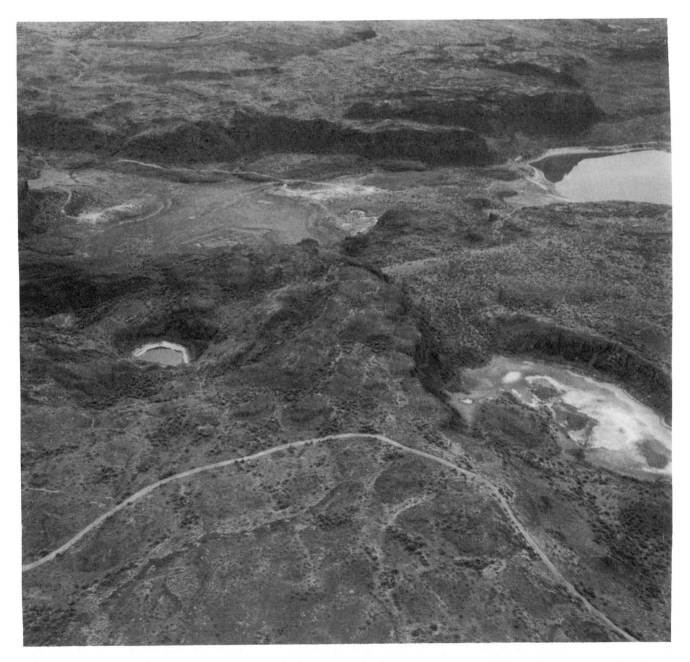

Photo Courtesy of Odessa Economic Development Committee

This aerial photo shows the flood-scoured landscape created by the two-week-long 600-foot-deep waters of the Missoula Flood.

will take you into the **Coal Creek Coulee [6]**. Its walls have a lot of small basalt caves that were created when the floodwater pulled out large chunks of rock.

Follow Lamona Road south 7 miles and you'll see Crab Creek. To the east, an upright columnade marks the bottom of the **Roza Flow [7]**. Head west on Laney Road to get back to Odessa. This route offers a good view of the floodway. Imagine this gorge filled to the top with bubbling lava, and again with ice-filled water.

More Ice Age scenery can be seen west of Odessa. Drive 10 miles to Irby Road and turn north. Leaving the highway, you are at first traveling on lava from the Roza flow, then between columns formed during the **Frenchman Springs Flows [8]**.

Reaching the floor of Crab Creek, you are looking at cliffs created by the region's most catastrophic eruptions, the **Grand Ronde Basalt Flows [9]**. Standing here, you have 4,000 feet of lava from more than 100 separate flows beneath your feet. During the great flood, the water here was 300 feet deep.

The soil to the north resembles the loess that covered this entire region prior to the flood. This area was an isolated island during the flood, circled by a swirling mass of muddy water that was filled with huge chunks of ice, house-sized rocks and uprooted trees.

The Grand Coulee

Follow State Highways 21 and 174 north/northwest of Odessa to **Grand Coulee [10]**. This steep-walled chasm was created when the Ice Age Columbia River became blocked by glaciers, forc-

ing it across the lava field to where it could carve a new channel. The Grand Coulee is 50 miles long and up to 900 feet deep.

At the **Grand Coulee Dam [11]** visitors' center you can see how North America's largest hydroelectric dam was built, examine some of the artifacts found here, get information on local recreation, pick up a tour map, and take a 30-minute tour of the dam.

On summer evenings the dam serves as a backdrop for a laser light show, one of the world's largest. It features 300-foot-high animated images, beautifully accompanied by music and narrative, lasting about 40 minutes. From Memorial Day weekend through July the show begins at 10:00 p.m., in August it starts a half-hour earlier, and in September at 8:30 p.m. To get a good seat, be sure to arrive an hour early.

The building of this dam also created Lake Roosevelt, and more than 600 miles of recreational lakeshore. Managed as the **Lake Roosevelt National Recreation Area [12]**, these parklands provide public access to some beautiful high deserts, dense pine forests, a number of campgrounds and family parks.

Fishing on **Lake Roosevelt [13]** and nearby **Banks Lake [14]** is good year round. Bass, trout, kokanee, perch, crappie, whitefish, ling cod, sunfish, sturgeon and chinook salmon are all caught here.

Steamboat Rock State Park [15] is 8 miles south of Grand Coulee and centers on a flat-topped butte rising 1,000 feet above Banks Lake. The butte, Steamboat Rock, was once an island in

Photo Courtesy of U.S. Dept. of Interior/Grand Coulee Project Office

Grand Coulee Dam is North America's largest hydroelectric dam. Behind it, Lake Roosevelt provides vacationers with 600 miles of recreational lakeshore.

the ancient Columbia River. A trail to the top provides a panoramic view of the landscape and access to 640 quiet acres.

The **Banks Lake Wildlife Refuge [16]** is located mid-way between Electric City and Coulee City. It provides a safe haven for at least 16 kinds of waterfowl, including western grebe, great blue heron and the common loon, plus about 40 species of dryland birds.

The Largest Waterfall on Earth

About 4 miles southwest of Coulee City you'll find the most impressive of all the Ice Age Flood features, **Dry Falls [17]**. This was once the largest waterfall on earth. Water 300 feet deep raced over its rocky edge with such force that it shook the ground and created a roar that could have been heard 100 miles away.

At one time, this dry rim held a waterfall 3.5 times wider and 2.5 times higher than Niagara Falls. Nearly half of all the glacial floodwaters in North America thundered over this spot. Its 400 foot cliffs provide unshakable testimony to one of the most spectacular geologic events on our planet.

The Dry Falls Visitor Center is only open from the middle of May to late September, between 10:00 a.m. and 6:00 p.m. Inside you can watch a video on Ice Age Floods and view exhibits explaining the changes that have taken place here during the last 20 million years.

The largest waterfall on earth once thundered across this ridge. It was 3-1/2 times wider and 2-1/2 times higher than Niagara Falls and could be heard 100 miles away.

Outside, a viewpoint overlooks the now empty falls. During the summer you'll often find a ranger there to point out the landmark's special features. Hiking trails also allow for closer inspection.

The Dry Falls area is part of **Sun Lakes State Park [18]**. Besides camping facilities, this 3,365 acre park has 3 lakes, a tree shaded picnic grove, swimming beach and restrooms.

About 5 miles south of Sun Lakes State Park, along Highway 17, are the **Lake Lenore Caves [19]**. Created when melting glaciers forced chunks of basalt from the coulee walls, these tiny pocket caves are thought to have been used as temporary shelters by nomadic prehistoric hunters.

The summer temperature in eastern Washington is generally hot. However, between the **Columbia River [20]**, Lake Roosevelt, and other local lakes you'll find plenty of water to play in during your Ice Age vacation. To avoid sunstroke, do any strenuous hiking early in the day, and spend the afternoon inside, or around water.

A Petrified Forest

If your travels take you near the junction of I-90 and the Columbia River, on your way to or from your vacation, stop at Vantage for a look at the **Ginkgo Petrified Forest State Park [21]**. Once there, you can hike along a prehistoric lakebed where 20-million-year-old logs exist in petrified form.

This land was lush, with lots of trees and ferns, before volcanic eruptions created the Cascade Mountain Range. When the hot lava hit the swamp forest,

For Additional Information

The Odessa Visitor Information Center offers an easy-to-follow auto tour brochure showing the Ice Age features around this small town and provides a good base for in-depth explorations. For further information on other attractions call the agencies listed below.

Odessa Visitor Information
(509) 982-2232

Grand Coulee Dam Chamber of Commerce
(509) 633-3074 or (800) 268-5332

Lake Roosevelt National Recreation Area
(509) 633-9441

Dry Falls Visitor Center
(509) 632-5214

Sun Lakes State Park
(509) 632-5583

Ginkgo Petrified Forest State Park
(509) 856-2700

it formed molten rock pillows. Because the water smothered the heat, the plant life was not completely consumed. Instead, more than 200 different species of trees were petrified. The most unusual is the Ginkgo tree, a species that has been around for 250 million years.

The Native Americans who lived in this area used the petrified wood to make arrowheads and trinkets. They also created more than 300 petroglyphs near the current park site. Most were buried under **Wanapum Reservoir [22]**, but a few are on display at the park.

Stop at the Interpretive Center first, before following one of the two short hiking trails. The center offers a terrific slide show that explains the evolution of this area, as well as samples of the hundreds of different kinds of petrified wood found here. Budget problems have hit this site pretty hard, but you'll usually find the center open from mid-June to mid-September, between 10:00 a.m. and 6:00 p.m., Wednesday thru Sunday.

The Ginkgo Petrified Forest State Park also has a public swimming beach, boat launch and picnic facilities, down by the Columbia River.

Ice Age Area Accommodations

COULEE CITY

Ala Cozy Motel
(509) 632-5703
9988 US Highway 2E
10 rooms, outdoor pool, $35-65

Sun Village Resort
(509) 632-5664
33575 Park Lake Rd NE - Go 2 miles west on US Hwy. 2 and 8 miles south on State Hwy 17.
19 cabins w/bath & kitchen - singles to 4 bedroom, pets okay - $5 fee, family resort on lake, picnic/bbq area, deli, store, swimming, fishing, boat launch & rental, $44-97.

The Main Stay B&B
(509) 632-5687
110 W. Main
2 rooms w/private bath, no smoking, pets okay, disabled access, $40, includes continental breakfast.

COULEE DAM

Columbia River Cottage
(509) 633-2908
209 Columbia Ave.
Cottage w/pri. bath & hot tub, view of dam, ref., sleeps 2, $150 ($110).

Columbia River Inn
(800) 633-6421 or (509) 633-2100
10 Lincoln St.
34 units, river view rooms, outdoor swimming pool, year round outdoor hot tub, $49-95.

Coulee House Motel
(800) 715-7767 or (509) 633-1101
110 Roosevelt Way
61 rooms - some w/spa & view, handicap access, pool, pets okay, restaurant, located adjacent to the casino, $50-108.

Four Winds Guest House B&B
(800) 786-3146 or (509) 633-3146
301 Lincoln St.
10 rooms w/private baths, no pets or smoking, older children okay, $62-79, includes full breakfast.

GRAND COULEE

Center Lodge Motel
(509) 633-0770
508 Spokane Way
17 rooms & suites, kitchenettes available, no handicap access, pets okay, $45-75.

Gold House Inn B&B (800) 835-9369
411 Partello Park (509) 633-3276
7 rooms - 5 w/private bath, kids okay,
no pets or smoking, $50-90, includes
full breakfast.

Trail West Motel
(509) 633-3155
108 Spokane Way
26 rooms, kitchenettes, pets okay,
pool, no handicap access, $39-70.

MOSES LAKE

Best Western Hallmark Inn
(888) 448-4449 or (509) 765-9211
3000 W Marina Dr.
161 rooms, suites & jacuzzi rooms,
pets okay, handicap access, sauna,
pool, tennis, laundry, lake, boat docks,
fitness center, rest./lounge, $60-140.

IMA El Rancho Motel
(800) 341-8000 or (509) 765-9173
1214 S Pioneer Way
20 rooms, kitchens, pool, picnic area,
pets okay, $30-44.

Moses Lake Super 8 Motel
(800) 800-8000 or (509) 765-8886
49 Melva Lane
62 rooms & suites, handicap access,
spa, laundry, pets okay, $45-80.

Moses Lake Travelodge
(800) 578-7878 or (509) 765-8631
316 S Pioneer Way
40 rooms, pool, downtown, walk to
rest., small pets okay - $5 fee, $35-85.

ODESSA

Derr House B&B
(800) 469-0076
302 E First Ave.
3 rooms, no smoking or pets, $50-60,
includes full breakfast.

Odessa Motel
(509) 982-2412
609 E First Ave.
11 rooms, pets okay, $35-48.

RITZVILLE

Best Western Heritage Inn
(509) 659-1007
1513 Smittys Blvd.
42 rooms, pool, hot tub, pets okay,
handicap access, $47-145.

Colwell Motor Inn
(800) 341-8000 or (509) 659-1620
501 W First (I-90 exit #220)
25 ground level rooms, pets okay - fee,
bbq area, $35-65.

West Side Motel
(800) 559-1164
407 W First
11 rooms, pets okay, $28-46, includes
continental breakfast.

SOAP LAKE

Royal View Motel
(509) 246-1831
State Highway 17
19 rooms, across from lake, pets okay,
$39 and up.

The Inn @ Soap Lake
(509) 246-1132
226 Main Ave. E
28 rooms, pool, hot tub, exercise
room, $55-100, includes continental
breakfast.

Tolo Vista Cottage
(509) 246-1512
22 Daisy N
6 rooms, disabled access, $44 and up.

WILBUR

Eight Bar B Motel
(509) 647-2400
718 E Main
15 rooms, pool, pets okay, $30-65.

Settle Inn Motel
(509) 647-2100
303 NE Main
11 rooms, pets okay, $30-36.

Ice Age Area Campgrounds & RV Parks

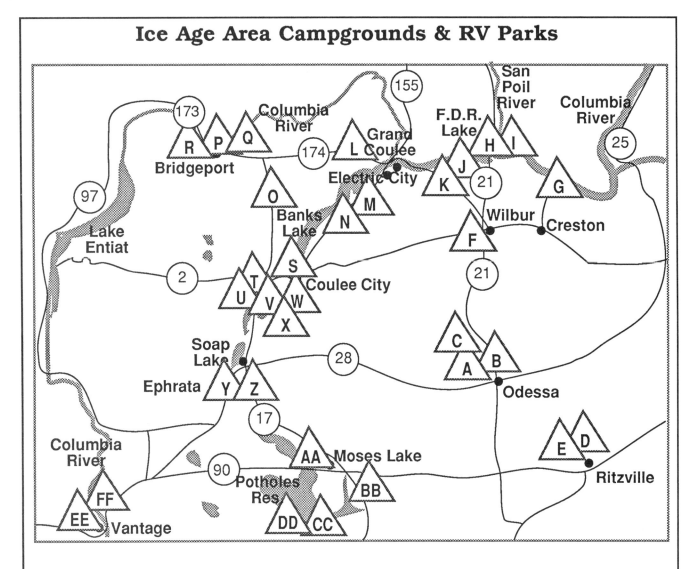

A) ODESSA GOLF CLUB RV PARK

12 units w/full hookups, reservations (509) 982-0093, on golf course, pets okay, $10/night. They have special rates for course golfers.

This RV park is right on the golf course, at the west end of Odessa.

B) REIMAN CITY PARK

Campsite area in Odessa city park - no fee, flush toilets, drinking water.

This park is located at the corner of First Avenue and Second Street.

C) LAKEVIEW BLM RANCH

Lakeview Ranch sports a large primitive campground area and covers 5,000 acres in the heart of Eastern Washington's Ice Age landscape. Chemical toilets, drinking water, horse & hiking trails, plentiful bird watching, horse corrals and a loading chute are available. Off-road vehicles are not allowed. There is no fee for overnight camping.

Located 3 miles north of Odessa. Follow State Highway 21 and turn at sign.

E) BEST WESTERN HERITAGE INN & RV PARK
30 RV/trailer sites w/full hookups, reservations (509) 659-1007, wheelchair access, showers, laundry, swimming pool, therapy spa, $20/night.

Leave I-90 at Ritzville on exit #221. This motel campground is located along the frontage road.

F) BELLS RV/MOBILE HOME PARK
30 trailer sites w/full hookups plus grassy area for tents, reservations (509) 647-5888, showers, laundry, picnic area, $10-14/night.

Located in Wilbur, at the east end of town; one block off US Hwy. 2.

G) HAWK CREEK LRNRA CAMPGROUND
28 campsites, trailers okay, no hookups, well water, lake, fishing, boat launch & dock, pets okay, $10/night.

Take US Hwy. 2 east of Wilbur to the town of Creston, then go north 17 miles to campground.

H) THE RIVER RUE RV PARK
85 units, 25 w/full hookups, 14 w/water & electricity, plus 46 tent sites, reservations (509) 647-2647, wheelchair access, showers, playground, trailer waste disposal, $12 to $17/night.

Located north of Wilbur 14 miles on State Hwy. 21.

I) KELLER FERRY LRNRA CAMPGROUND
50 units - trailers okay, no hookups, 2 group areas, picnic area, trailer & boat waste disposal, boat ramp & dock, swimming, $10/night - group sites $25.

Located north of Wilbur approximately 14 miles on State Hwy. 21.

J) SPRING CANYON LRNRA CAMP
78 campsites - trailers okay, plus primitive & boat-in camp, no hookups, drinking water, no reservations, information (509) 633-9188, picnic area, handicap access, beach, volleyball, playground, trailer & boat waste disposal, boat dock & ramp, swimming, pets okay, $10/night - primitive & boat-in campsites are free.

Take State Hwy. 174 southeast of Grand Coulee 5 miles to campground road and follow north 1.1 miles.

K) KING'S COURT RV PARK
28 campsites w/full hookups, showers, handicap access, showers, laundry, pets okay, $15 to $20/night.

Located in Grand Coulee at the junction of State Hwy. 174 and Grand Coulee Ave. E.

K) LAKEVIEW TERRACE RV PARK
20 units w/full hookups plus group tent area, pull thrus, information (509) 633-2169, showers, laundry, picnic area, wheelchair access, pets okay, playground, $10 and up/night.

Located southeast of Grand Coulee 3 miles on State Hwy. 174.

L) GRAND COULEE RV PARK
26 campsites - 10 w/full hookups plus 16 tent units, information (509) 633-0750, showers, picnic area, trailer waste disposal, pets okay, $9 to $15/night.

Located northwest of Grand Coulee 2 miles at 22718 State Hwy. 174 E.

M) COULEE PLAYLAND RESORT & RV PARK
65 campsites, 40 w/full hookups, 13 w/water & electricity, plus 12 tent sites, information (509) 633-2671, showers, laundry, on Banks Lake, playground, trailer waste disposal, swimming, fishing, boat launch, boat rental, $16 to $18/night.

Take State Hwy. 155 west of Grand Coulee 1 mile.

M) SUN BANKS RESORT
250 campsites w/full hookups - tents okay, on Banks Lake, showers, handi-

cap access, pets okay, laundry, store, trailer waste disposal, boat launch, swimming beach, boat rentals, $10 to $23/night.

Located south of Electric City on State Hwy. 155 S.

N) STEAMBOAT ROCK STATE PARK
112 campsites w/full hookups plus 82 tent & group campsites, reservations (800) 452-5687, information (509) 633-1304, wheelchair access, pets okay, located on Banks Lake, trailer waste disposal, showers, playground, boat launch, fishing, water skiing, scuba diving, $10 to $16/night.

Take State Hwy. 155 southwest of Grand Coulee 7.2 miles.

O) BLUE LAKE RESORT
100 campsites - 23 w/full hookups, 33 w/water & elec., 44 tent units, plus 10 cabins w/kitchens, reservations (509) 632-5364, showers, groceries, fishing tackle, pets okay, playfield, playground, lake, swimming, fishing, boat launch & rental, camping - $15/night - cabins $34-69.

Take US Hwy. 2 west of Coulee City 2 miles, and follow State Hwy. 17 south 10 miles to resort.

P) WATERFRONT MARINA CITY CAMPGROUND
43 trailer sites - 18 w/full hookups, 4 w/water & elec., 1 handicap RV site, plus 20 dry sites, showers, picnic area, pets okay, playground, trailer waste disposal, river fishing, boat launch & dock, $11 to $16/night.

Located in Bridgeport, at Columbia Avenue & 7th Street.

Q) BRIDGEPORT STATE PARK
34 units - 20 w/water & electricity, plus 14 tent sites, trailers to 45', wheelchair accessible, on Lake Rufus Woods, trailer waste disposal, boat launch, fishing, open April thru Oct., $10 to $16/night.

At Bridgeport take State Hwy. 173 to State Hwy. 17. Head north 1.5 miles.

R) BIG RIVER RV PARK
16 units w/full hookups plus grassy tent area, reservations (509) 686-2121, trailers to 40', showers, laundry, propane, on Columbia River, fishing, no pets, open year round, $7 to $14/night.

Located in Bridgeport, at 1415 Jefferson.

S) COULEE CITY PARK
140 campsites, 34 w/full hookups, plus 106 tent units, trailers to 24', information (509) 632-5331, showers, playground, trailer waste disposal, lake swimming, fishing, boat launch, pets okay, $9 to $12/night.

Located in Coulee City, at the north end of town.

T) SUN LAKES STATE PARK
193 units, 18 w/full hookups, no fire pits, wheelchair access, trailer waste disposal, boat & horse rental, boat launch, fishing, swimming, horse trails, pets okay, $15 to $16/night.

Take US Hwy. 2 west of Coulee City 2 miles, then follow State Hwy. 17 south 5 miles.

U) SUN LAKES PARK RESORT
59 trailer sites w/full hookups, tents okay, no fire pits, information (509) 632-5291, showers, handicap access, laundry, groceries, pets okay, trailer waste disposal, swimming pool, playfield, lake, fishing, boat launch & rental, golf & mini golf, hiking, $16 and up/night.

Take US Hwy. 2 west of Coulee City 2 miles, then follow State Hwy. 17 south 7 miles.

V) LAURENTS SUN VILLAGE RESORT
124 units - 56 w/hookups, 40 w/water & elec. plus 28 tent sites, (509) 632-5664, pull-thrus, pets okay, showers, handicap access, laundry, picnic area, lake, boat rentals, boat dock & launch, swimming, water skiing, playground, fishing, hiking, $16 and up/night.

Follow US Hwy. 2 west of Coulee City 2 miles, State Hwy. 17 south 8 miles, and Park Lake Rd. northeast 1 mile.

W) COULEE LODGE RESORT
52 units - 22 w/full hookups, 11 w/water & elec., plus 19 tent sites, information (509) 632-5565, wheelchair access, pets okay, showers, laundry, trailer waste disposal, lake, swimming, fishing, boat launch, boat rental, $13 and up/night.

Take US Hwy. 2 west of Coulee City 2 miles, then follow State Hwy. 17 south 8 miles.

X) SUN VILLAGE RESORT
115 campsites - 95 w/full hookups plus 20 w/water & electricity, tents okay, information (509) 632-5664, showers, laundry, groceries, playground, trailer waste disposal, pets okay - $5 fee, lake, swimming, fishing, boat launch & rental, $16/night.

Take US Hwy. 2 west of Coulee City 2 miles and State Hwy. 17 south 8 miles.

Y) OASIS PARK
69 campsites - 28 w/full hookups, 41 w/water & electricity, plus big tent area, reservations (509) 754-5102, wheelchair access, showers, laundry, covered picnic area, pool, golf & mini golf, playfield, trailer waste disposal, swimming, fishing, hiking, pets okay, $10 to $16/night.

Located in Ephrata.

Z) SOAP LAKES SMOKIAM CITY CAMPGROUND
52 campsites w/full hookups, tents okay, showers, groceries, laundry, trailer waste disposal, playground, lake swimming, fishing, Soap Lake mud baths, pets okay, $7 to $10/night.

Located northwest of Moses Lake about 26 miles via State Hwy. 17.

AA) BIG SUN RESORT
50 campsites w/full hookups, plus 10 tent sites, reservations (509) 765-8294, showers, laundry, playground, on Moses Lake, boat launch & rental, $12 to $18/night.

Located in Moses Lake. Leave I-90 at exit #176 and take Broadway north .5 mile. Campground is west, at 2300 W. Marina Drive.

AA) SUN CREST RESORT
90 campsites w/full hookups plus grassy tent area, reservations (509) 765-0355, trailers to 52', pull thrus, showers, pets okay, laundry, wheelchair access, swimming pool, jacuzzi, game room, playground, open year round, $15-24 - memberships also available.

Take the Hansen Rd. exit off I-90 and go to 303 N. Hansen Rd.

BB) WILLOWS TRAILER VILLAGE
64 sites, 38 w/full hookups, 8 w/water & electricity, plus large tent area, reservations (509) 765-7531, showers, laundry, playfield, trailer waste disposal, pets okay, $13 to $17/night.

Take State Hwy. 17 south of I-90 for 2 miles, and CR M southeast .3 mile.

CC) MAR DON RESORT
350 sites, 160 w/full hookups, 55 w/water & elec., 135 w/out hookups, plus beach tent area & motel rooms, reservations (509) 765-5061, pets okay - $5 fee, showers, playground, tackle shop & store, on Potholes Reservoir, marina, boat moorage, fishing dock, boat launch, swimming beach, hiking, $16 to $19/night.

Follow State Hwy. 17 south of I-5 10 miles, and Potholes Reservoir Road west 8 miles.

DD) POTHOLES STATE PARK
126 units - 60 w/full hookups, plus 66 tent sites, wheelchair accessible trails, trailer waste disposal, on Potholes Reservoir, boat launch, fishing, water skiing, pets okay, $10 to $16/night.

Take State Hwy. 17 south of I-5 10 miles, then Potholes Reservoir Road west 13 miles.

EE) VANTAGE KOA

150 units, 100 w/full hookups - 14 pull-thrus, plus 36 tent sites & 1 cabin, (509) 856-2230, showers, laundry, groceries, rec room, playground, swimming pool, trailer waste disposal, on Columbia River, fishing, pets okay, $17 to $22/night - cabin $30/2 people.

Located in Vantage, 2 blocks north of I-90's exit #136.

FF) GINKGO/WANAPUM STATE PARK

50 campsites w/full hookups, in Ginkgo Petrified Forest, boat launch, fishing, beach access, hiking trail, pets okay, $15/night.

Located north of the town of Vantage. Take I-90 east 1 mile to park exit.

Vacation #7

The Best of the Columbia River Gorge

Multnomah Falls is the *Queen of the Gorge* waterfalls. At 620 feet tall, it is the United States' second highest waterfall. In all, nine waterfalls can be seen from the Columbia River Scenic Highway.

FROM THE AUTHOR'S JOURNAL . . .

Having spent most of my life in the Portland area, I've explored the Columbia River Gorge pretty thoroughly.

My out-of-state visitors always got the standard waterfall tour, and if they were the kind of people who appreciate art and history they were taken to Maryhill and Stonehenge. Whenever I was looking for a close-in hike, I always knew I could find some place special by heading up the gorge.

Now it's a national treasure. There are more out-of-state license plates than local, and visiting windsurfers have overrun its once quiet beaches. But the Columbia River Gorge still retains some of the special qualities that have always brought me here. I just have to look a little harder.

Since most Gorge visitors are just driving through, or are there only to ride the wind and water, those of us who are looking for a less crowded experience only have to travel inland to get away from most of the congestion.

Off-season travel is also a good way to avoid the vacationing masses. The waterfalls are at their best in the spring, and Oneonta Gorge has very few visitors in the fall. And when it comes to hiking, I've found that any trail longer than four miles is beyond the energy of most casual visitors, any time of the year.

Thoughts on avoiding the crowds that the fame of being a National Recreation Area has brought to the Columbia River Gorge

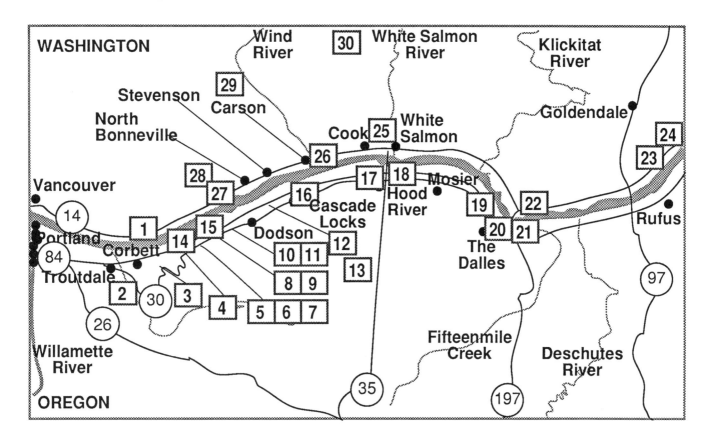

Columbia River Gorge Attractions

The **Columbia River Gorge National Scenic Area [1]** begins 16 miles east of Portland, and includes land on both sides of the river. It preserves a lush, water-filled canyon that nature has cut through the Cascade Mountains, and is lined with breathtaking waterfalls, impressive forests and sheer basalt cliffs.

Because of its proximity to Portland, and its national recreational status, the gorge is sometimes overrun with people. But even those seeking solitude can find happiness, if they just spend a little time researching the area.

Within the scenic area three bridges span the Columbia River, providing easy access to attractions on both sides. The bridges are found at Oregon's Cascade Locks, Hood River and The Dalles.

The **Columbia River Scenic Highway [2]** runs between Troutdale and The Dalles, just south of I-84. Built between 1913 and 1925, it originally covered 83 miles, traveling over creeks and rivers, around foothills, and right through towering basalt cliffs. This colossal endeavor was constructed entirely by hand. Nearly 60 miles of the original route is maintained, providing travelers with spectacular views, trail access, and the opportunity to view several waterfalls.

Following this highway, most visitors make their first stop after 5 miles, at **Crown Point Vista House [3]**. Built in 1918, this historic stone structure is perched high above the river and offers an expansive view. Inside, you'll find historic memorabilia as well as a nice little gift shop and public restrooms.

An Abundance of Waterfalls

Heading east, you'll travel past nine waterfalls. The first, 224' **Latourelle Falls [4]**, was originally called Was-ke-wa by the region's Native Americans. According to legend, the falls were formed when the creator, Speelyie, threw one of his wives over the mountains. Her hair is represented by the water. Today it carries the name of a pioneer family.

At **Sheppard's Dell [5]**, Young's Creek drops into a quiet cove. It can be viewed from the bridge, or you can take the stairs down for a closer look.

Logging has destroyed most of **Bridal Veil Falls [6]** power and beauty. You'll find what's left of it beneath the bridge at the village of Bridal Veil.

Mist Falls [7] is splendid, and the 242' **Wahkeena Falls [8]** is actually a series of waterfalls. Wah-ke-nah is an Indian word meaning "most beautiful", and this spot is appropriately named. The upper falls are known as Little Fairy and Ghost Falls.

Next, you'll come to the gorge's most famous feature, **Multnomah Falls [9]**. At 620', it is the United States' second highest waterfall and accessible from both the scenic highway and I-84. It's a short stroll to the bottom of the falls, and an easy hike to the bridge viewpoint. If you've got the energy, hike toward the top for a panoramic view.

Be sure to check out the historic Multnomah Falls Lodge while you're there. Its walls are said to contain samples of every kind of rock found within the Columbia River Gorge.

Follow Highway 30 east of Multnomah Falls 25 miles to explore **Oneonta Gorge [10]**. This picturesque crevice was created by an ancient earthquake. Follow the creek back and you'll find a lovely, secluded waterfall. This little treasure is reached by wading the creek.

In the late summer, when the water is low, wading the creek provides a wonderful family adventure. It doesn't take long, and is a great way to beat the heat. The water is very shallow this time of year, and there is very little current.

Horsetail Falls [11] is just a short distance beyond Oneonta Gorge. One look at this 208' cascade is all you need to understand why it was so named. **Elowah Falls [12]** drops 289' at McCord Creek, and dozens of lesser known waterfalls are found in the hills.

Hiking Trails & Windsurfing Beaches

The **Mt. Hood National Forest [13]** covers a vast area south of the river, and provides hikers with a wealth of trails. The gorge section alone has more than 150 miles of trails. These will lead you off the beaten path, rewarding your efforts with unsurpassable views and a chance to enjoy those hidden waterfalls.

Stop at the forest service office in Troutdale for personal help in finding the right trail. Beginners should ask about the Latourelle Falls, Multnomah-Wahkeena Loop, and Elowah Falls

Oneonta Gorge was created by a giant earthquake. If you hike up the creek, you'll find a lovely, secluded waterfall.

Trails. Experienced hikers will enjoy the more difficult Ruckel Creek Trails, or the one up Nick Eaton Ridge. If you really want a workout, check out either the Gorton Creek Trail or the one up Mt. Defiance.

Windsurfing is extremely popular in the gorge. In fact, Hood River is considered the windsurfing capital of the Northwest. **Rooster Rock State Park [14], Dalton Point [15]** and **Cascade Locks Park [16]** are hot, as is the **Hood River**

Marina [17], **Koberg Beach [18]** and **Mayer State Park [19]**. The Dalles' **Riverfront Park [20]** is popular with beginners.

You can take a free train ride at **The Dalles Dam [21]**. It operates May thru September, every half hour from 10:00 a.m. to 5:00 p.m. At the end of the ride you can watch as fish make their way up the fish ladders, tour the powerhouse, see the massive generators, and learn how the river is used to create power.

Before the dam's construction, the rock cliffs here contained more than 400 ancient Indian petroglyphs and pictographs. A few were removed before the rising waters buried them, and are on display at the dam.

The Washington Shore

Cross the river at The Dalles and head east on Highway 14. You'll find more pictographs among the rocks at **Horsethief Lake State Park [22]**, 2 miles east of Highway 14's junction with Highway 197. Park by the west boat ramp and take the path on the right to view the ancient artwork. A family picnic area is also available at the park.

Continue east a short distance on Highway 14 for an opportunity to tour Eastern Washington's finest art museum. The **Maryhill Art Museum [23]** is housed in a stately old mansion, surrounded by miles of sparsely populated desert.

Maryhill's displays include Rodin sculptures, colorful Russian icons, ornate Rumanian furnishings, Native American art and artifacts, Galle art glass and other rare treats. You'll also find one-of-a-kind collections, including the elegantly dressed *Theatre de la Mode* miniature Parisian fashion mannequins and over 100 antique chess sets. The museum is open from March 15th to November 15th, 9:00 a.m. to 5:00 p.m., and is a real bargain at about $4.00 for adults, $1.50 for kids.

Just east of the museum you can see a full-size replica of England's Stonehenge. Perched on a bluff, overlooking the Columbia, this **Stonehenge [24]** was built in remembrance of local residents killed during World War I. It was the United States' first WWI memorial. At the time of construction, the original Stonehenge was thought to have been a sacrificial site, a fact the builder found to be a fitting accolade to war.

Heading back along the Washington shore, State Highway 14 follows much of the route taken by Lewis and Clark during their famous expedition.

September is the best time of year to see the large chinook salmon at **Spring Creek Fish Hatchery [25]**. They rear about 17 million fingerlings here each year, and allow visitors between 7:30 a.m. and 4:00 p.m. Monday thru Friday during the summer, and daily the rest of the year. To get there, leave State Highway 14 about 2 miles west of White Salmon and follow the signs.

Windsurfers frequent **Home Valley Park [26]**, the public beaches around Stevenson and North Bonneville, and the waters west of US Highway 97. Summer winds generally blow 20-30 mph, and a variety of conditions can be found. Even if you don't ride the waves, it's fun to watch.

You don't have to go to England to ponder the question of Stonehenge. A full-sized replica stands along the Columbia River east of Goldendale, Washington.

Beacon Rock [27] is hard to miss, on the shore of the Columbia River west of Stevenson. A steep trail winds upward 900 feet, providing hikers with a birds-eye view of the gorge. The trail is not difficult, but it is steep, so you'll need to wear good shoes and allow plenty of time. The view is well worth the effort.

If you've got any energy left after climbing up and down Beacon Rock, cross the highway to Beacon Rock State Park and take the **Hamilton Mountain Trail [28]**. It will lead you over Rodney and Hardy Falls.

Exploring Gifford Pinchot National Forest

Two of the Gifford Pinchot National Forest's prettiest districts are found just north of the Columbia River. **Wind River Valley [29]**, north of Carson, and the **Trout Lake Area [30]** are both fun to explore.

The Dalles Dam has los of fun things to do. You can take a free ride on the train, visit the duckpond, count fish as they make their way up the fish ladder, and learn how the river is used to create power. The huge generators shown here are located in the powerhouse.

In the Wind River district, the Paradise Trail will lead you through old growth conifers for a beautiful view of the upper valley.

The Falls Creek Trail has a couple of nice waterfalls, and the Lower Falls Creek Trail takes you over the water on a log-stringer bridge. The Siouxon and Chinook Trails also lead to waterfalls.

Stop at the Wind River ranger's office in Carson for directions. Or better yet, contact the Gifford Pinchot National Forest headquarters when planning your trip for maps and information.

The Trout Lake area is reached via State Highway 141, west of White Salmon. Deadhorse, Dry Creek, Cheese and Ice Caves are in this district, along with numerous hiking trails and berry fields. The Mt. Adams ranger station, in Trout Lake, is the best place to find out more about the caves, and which trails fit your skills and schedule.

For Additional Information

The following agencies can provide you with detailed maps and information on Columbia River Gorge attractions. Request anything they have about the area, and you'll discover lots of out-of-the way sights that won't be too crowded. The Oregon State Parks department, for example, has a wonderful brochure showing lots of gorge trails.

Columbia River Gorge National Scenic Area
(541) 386-2333

Oregon State Parks
(800) 452-5687
from Portland call 731-3411

Washington State Parks
(800) 233-0321

Mt. Hood National Forest
(503) 668-1700

Gifford Pinchot National Forest
(360) 891-5000

Maryhill Art Museum
(509) 773-3733

Hood River Chamber of Commerce
(541) 386-2000

The Dalles Visitors Info Center
(541) 296-6616

Columbia River Gorge Area Accommodations

OREGON ACCOMMODATIONS

CASCADE LOCKS

Best Western Columbia River Inn
(800) 595-7108 or (541) 374-8777
735 WaNaPa St.
62 rooms w/microwave & ref., indoor pool & spa, pets okay, handicap access, $54-129.

Bridge of the Gods Motel
630 WaNaPa St. (541) 374-8628
8 units, some w/kitchens, river views, laundry, walk to restaurants, $36-60.

Econo Inn (541) 374-8417
Columbia Gorge Center
30 units, Scandinavian style, $29-48, handicap access, lounge, walk to restaurant & laundry.

HOOD RIVER

Avalon B&B (541) 386-2520
3444 Avalon Dr.
3 rooms in renovated 1906 farmhouse, shared bath, near river, view of Mt. Adams, $50-65, inc. full breakfast, no smoking or pets indoors.

Beryl House B&B (541) 386-5567
4079 Barrett Dr.
4 rooms in homey 1910 farmhouse surrounded by pear orchard, mountain views, inc. full breakfast, wheelchair access, pets okay, $60-70.

Best Western Hood River Inn
(800) 828-7873 or (541) 386-2200
1108 E Marina Way
149 units, on Columbia River, views, pets okay, handicap access, pool & spa, restaurant/lounge, $49-165.

Brown's B&B (541) 386-1545
3000 Reed Road
2 rooms in quiet hillside farmhouse, mountain view, hiking trails, no-smoking, no pets or small children, $45-65, inc. gourmet breakfast.

Cascade Avenue B&B
823 Cascade Ave. (541) 387-2377
2 rooms in antique-furnished English cottage, downtown, inc. gourmet breakfast, gorge view, no smoking.

Columbia Gorge Hotel
(800) 345-1921 or (541) 386-5566
4000 Westcliff Dr.
42 units in historic 1921 hotel, inc. breakfast, on bluff overlooking Columbia River, handicap access, pets okay, restaurant/lounge, $170-270.

Comfort Suites (800) 228-5150
2625 Cascade Ave. (541) 308-1000
62 suites w/microwave & ref., some w/jacuzzi, inc. cont. breakfast, indoor pool & spa, fitness center, sauna, handicap access, $69-129.

Cottonwood B&B (541) 386-1310
224 13th St.
5 rooms in Victorian-style home, private bath, inc. breakfast, near downtown, no smoking, kids okay, $50-80.

Gorge View B&B (541) 386-5770
1009 Columbia St. - May-Oct. only
3 rooms in 1917 Victorian home, inc. gourmet breakfast, hot tub, mountain views, walk to downtown, $35-70.

Hackett House B&B (541) 386-1014
922 State St.
4 rooms, pri. bath avail., inc. gourmet breakfast, near restaurants, $45-80.

Hood River Hotel (800) 386-1859
102 Oak St. (541) 386-1900
30 units & kitchen suites in 1913 vintage hotel, river views, downtown, jacuzzi, sauna, exercise facilities, handicap access, pets okay, restaurant/lounge, $49-145.

Inn at the Gorge B&B (541) 386-4429
1113 Eugene St. - Summer only
3 rooms w/pri. bath in Victorian home, separate entrance, kitchen, no smoking, $62-78, includes breakfast.

Inn at Orchard B&B (541) 354-2323
3801 Straight Hill Rd.
2 rooms, working orchard, no smoking/pets, $60, inc. gourmet breakfast.

Lakecliff Estate B&B (541) 386-7000
3820 Westcliff Dr.
May thru mid-September only.
4 rooms in 1908 summer home, private bath available, inc. gourmet breakfast, view of Columbia River, on National Register of Historic Places, large rooms, stone fireplace, $90-110.

Love's Riverview Lodge
(800) 789-9568 or (541) 386-8719
1505 Oak St.
20 rooms & suites, some w/ref. & microwaves, handicap access, pool & spa, no pets, $49-72.

Meredith Gorge Motel
4300 Westcliff Dr. (541) 386-1515
21 rooms - some w/kitchen, overlooks Columbia River, pets okay, walk to restaurants, $34-54.

Oak Street Hotel (541) 386-3845
610 Oak St.
9 rooms, $44-65, riverview rooms, handicap access, walk to restaurants.

Panorama Lodge (541) 387-2687
2290 Old Dalles Dr. - April-Oct. only
4 rooms in rustic log home, $45-75, views of Mt. Hood & Hood River Valley, no smoking or pets, children okay.

Prater's Motel (541) 386-3511
1306 Oak St.
7 rooms, $43-54, river views, handicap access, no pets, walk to downtown.

Skyline House B&B (541) 386-5141
5520 Skyline Dr.
4 rooms - 2 w/pri. bath in country, views of Mt. Hood & Hood River Valley, no smoking or pets, children okay, $80-125 ($75-100).

Sunset Motel (541) 386-6027
2300 W Cascade Ave.
14 rooms - some w/Gorge views, handicap access, laundry, no smoking or pets, $50-70.

Vagabond Lodge (541) 386-2992
4070 Westcliff Dr.
40 units in park-like setting, on cliff overlooking Columbia River, handicap access, playground, pets okay, walk to restaurants & shopping, $39-69.

THE DALLES

Best Western Umatilla House
Second & Liberty (541) 296-9107
65 rooms, jacuzzi suites, view, downtown, indoor pool, health club, pet friendly, $44-73.

Days Inn (800) DAYS INN
2500 W Sixth (541) 296-1191
70 rooms, inc. cont. breakfast, outdoor pool & hot tub, nearby restaurant, handicap access, pets okay, $37-54.

Guest House @ Stone House Farm
6700 Mill Creek Rd. (541) 296-6656
3 room cottage sleeps 4-7, includes kitchen, laundry, sport court, pond, creek, horse corral & trails, no smoking or pets, great family place, $60 ($300/week).

Quality Inn (800) 228-5151
2114 W Sixth St. (541) 298-5161
85 rooms - some w/kitchens, outdoor pool, restaurant/lounge, handicap access, $49-79.

Shilo Inn (800) 222-2244
3223 Clodfelter Way (541 298-5502
112 rooms & suites, inc. continental breakfast, pool, indoor spa & fitness center, restaurant/lounge, $69-115.

WASHINGTON ACCOMMODATIONS

BINGEN

Bingen School Inn Hostel
Humbolt & Cedar St. (509) 493-3363
9 rooms - largest sleeps 16, kitchen
facilities, lounge, equipment rentals,
indoor gym w/basketball hoop & rock
climbing wall, $11-30.

City Center Motel (509) 493-2445
205 Steuben
9 rooms - kitchens available, $35-44.

The Bingen Haus (509) 493-4888
706 W Steuben
6 rooms, pets okay, hot tub, spa, $40-
85, inc. full breakfast.

CARSON

Carson Hot Springs (509) 427-8292
1 St. Martin Rd.
9 rooms & suite in 1901 hotel plus 12
rustic cabins - some w/kitchen, RV
park, pets okay, disabled access,
restaurant, mineral water bathhouses,
massage, golf course, $43-60 (private
mineral bath suite w/kitchen $115).

Columbia Gorge Motel
1261 Wind River Rd. (509) 427-7777
10 room plus cottage w/acreage, pets
okay, $45-65.

GOLDENDALE

Barchris Motel (888)713-6197
128 N Academy
9 rooms, dis., pets okay, $35-42.

Far Vue Motel (800) 358-5881
808 E Simcoe Dr. (509) 773-5881
48 rooms, pool, disabled access, riding
arena, restaurant, $49-121.

Pine Springs Resort
2471 US Hwy. 97 (509) 773-4434
3 rooms plus tent & RV spaces, rooms
$50 and up, includes full breakfast.

Ponderosa Motel (509) 773-5842
775 E Broadway St.
28 rooms, pets okay, $36-70.

Victorian House B&B
415 E. Broadway (509) 773-5338
5 rooms in lovely 1910 home, $40-60,
includes full breakfast.

STEVENSON

Econo Lodge (800) 553-2666
40 NE Second St. (509) 427-5628
30 rooms, downtown, disabled access,
$45-65, inc. cont. breakfast.

Skamania Lodge (800) 221-7117
Stevenson (509) 427-7700
suites & rooms - some w/fireplace in
rustic mountain retreat, pool, handicap access, outdoor whirlpool, fitness
center, golf, tennis, restaurant, $135-
240 ($110-195).

The Timbers (509) 427-5656
200 SW Cascade
8 rooms, hot tub, spa, boat launch,
swimming, $75-200.

WHITE SALMON

Inn of the White Salmon
(800) 972-5226 or (509) 493-2335
172 W Jewett Blvd.
16 rooms in European-style B&B
hotel, some w/private bath, $99-115,
inc. full breakfast, pets & children
okay, outdoor hot tub, some rooms
w/view of Mt. Hood.

Columbia River Gorge Campgrounds & RV Parks

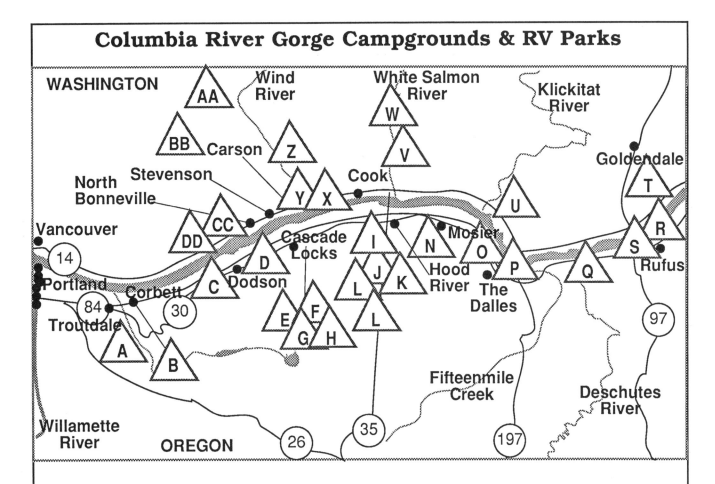

OREGON CAMPGROUNDS

A) OXBOW REGIONAL PARK
45 sites, trailers to 30', no hookups, information (503) 663-4708, pit toilets, fire pits, drinking water, river, fishing, boat launch, playfield, playground, wheelchair access, hiking, no pets, $13 for 1st/night – $10 additional nights. Gates locked from sunset to 6:30 a.m.!

East of Portland 8 miles on Division.

B) CROWN POINT RV PARK
20 trailer sites w/full hookups, plus a few tent sites, information (503) 695-5207, showers, laundry, trailer waste disposal, pets okay, $15 to $20/night.

East of Corbett .2 mile, on US Hwy. 30, near milepost #9.

C) AINSWORTH STATE PARK
45 units w/full hookups plus walk-in sites, maximum site 60', picnic area, showers, trailer waste disposal, hiking,

access to Columbia Gorge Trail, $4-18/night, campground host Mr.-Nov.

Located at junction of State Hwy. 3, US Hwy. 30's scenic route and I-84.

D) FISHERY - COVERTS LANDING
15 sites w/elec., tents okay, reservations (541) 374-8577, showers, wheelchair access, trailer waste disp., boat launch/moorage, $10 to $14/night.

Take exit #35 off I-84 at Dodson and follow signs to campground.

E) EAGLE CREEK CRGNSA CAMP
19 units, group area - reservations (541) 386-2333, trailers to 22', flush toilets, wheelchair access, creek, fishing, hiking, bicycling, in CRGNSA, pets okay, $8/night - groups $40 to $80.

Leave I-84 4.5 miles west of Cascade Locks, go east on I-84 2 miles, then follow FSR 240 southeast .1 mile.

F) CASCADE LOCKS MARINE PARK

45 campsites, no hookups, trailers to 35', tents okay, reservations (541) 374-8619, showers, trailer waste disposal, river, fishing, boat launch, museum, horseshoe pit, volleyball area, playground, wheelchair access, wind surfing, $8/night.

Located 3 blocks north of Cascade Locks exit off I-84.

G) BRIDGE OF THE GODS RV PARK

15 sites w/full hookups, trailers to 35', no tents, reservations (541) 374-8628, showers, laundry, tv hookup, fishing, $15/night.

In Cascade Locks, on US Hwy 30, right before the bridge.

H) CASCADE LOCKS KOA

78 campsites, 40 w/full hookups, 38 w/water & electricity, plus 9 cabins, tents welcome, reservations (541) 374-8668, showers, laundry, playground, pool, trailer waste disposal, pets okay, $18 to $23/night - cabins $30-36.

Located at the east end of Cascade Locks; take Forest Lane southeast 1 mile to campground.

I) WYETH FS CAMP

20 campsites plus 3 group areas, trailers to 31', flush toilets, drinking water, overlooks Columbia River, $7/night.

Located west of Hood River about 10 miles via I-84.

I) VIENTO STATE PARK

75 campsites - 58 w/electricity plus 17 tent units, maximum site 30', handicap access, no reservations - information (541) 374-8811, picnic area, showers, stream, hiking, $13 to $16/night, open Mr.-Nov, 100' elev.

West of Hood River 8 miles on I-84.

J) TUCKER COUNTY PARK

46 campsites - 18 w/water & electricity plus 28 tent sites, trailers to 30' w/hookups - no limit w/out, on Hood River, handicap access, reservations (541) 386-4477, showers, playfield & playground, picnic shelter, pets okay, fishing, $13 to $14/night, elev. 500'.

South of Hood River 6 miles on Tucker Road (State Hwy. 281).

K) ROUTSON COUNTY PARK

20 tent sites - not recommended for trailers, on Hood River, information (541) 386-6323, flush toilets, stream, fishing, pets okay, $5/night, elev. 2500'.

South of Hood River on State Hwy. 35 about 7 miles.

L) KINGSLEY RESERVOIR CTY. CG

20 tent sites, no drinking water, pit toilets, lake, boat ramp, fishing, hiking & mountain biking, in Mt. Hood NF, pets okay, no fee, elev. 3200'.

South of Hood River take FSR N20 for 12 miles to campground.

M) TOLL BRIDGE COUNTY PARK

80 campsites, 20 w/full hookups, 44 w/water & elec., plus 16 tent sites, showers, wheelchair access, trailer waste disposal, reservations (541) 352-5522, playfield, playground, hiking, river, fishing, pets okay, $13 to $14/night, elev. 1600'.

South of Hood River 18 miles on State Hwy. 35.

N) COLUMBIA RIVER GORGE RESORT

350 campsites, 250 w/water & electricity, plus 100 tent sites, reservations (541) 478-3750, showers, pool, sport court, picnic area, par 3 golf course, laundry, play area, wheelchair access, trailer waste disposal, pond fishing, swimming, hiking, spa, $14 to $18/night.

Located in Mosier, at 2350 Carroll Road.

O) MEMALOOSE STATE PARK

110 campsites, 43 w/full hookups, plus 67 tent units, maximum site 60', information (541) 478-3008, reservations (800) 551-6949, wheelchair access, showers, trailer waste disposal, $11 to $19/night, open Mr.-Nov.

Situated west of The Dalles 11 miles via I-84 - only accessible from westbound lanes of I-84.

P) LONE PINE RV PARK & MOTEL

22 trailer sites w/full hookups, no tents, information (541) 298-2800, reservations (800) 955-9626, showers, laundry, river, fishing, playground, $20/night.

Located in The Dalles, near the north end of I-84's exit #87 overpass.

Q) DESCHUTES RIVER STATE PARK

89 primitive sites plus 4 group camp areas, information (541) 739-2322, reservations (800) 551-6949, trailers to 30', picnic area, boating, fishing, hiking, $13 to $15/night, open year round.

Located east of The Dalles 17 miles via I-84.

R) LEPAGE PARK

20 sites w/water & elec. plus weekend/holiday tent area, some pull thrus, showers, trailer waste disposal, on John Day River, swimming area, fishing, boat launch, pets okay, $10 to $14/night.

Take I-84 east of Rufus 4 miles and follow the signs.

S) BOB'S BUDGET RV

26 units w/full hookups plus 10 tent sites, showers, handicap access, pull thrus to 60', reservations (541) 739-2272, laundry, pets okay, $10 to $15/night.

Take Rufus exit #109 to Old Highway 30, then go west .5 mile to Wallace Street, and .2 mile south.

WASHINGTON CAMPGROUNDS

T) SUNSET RV PARK

33 units w/full hookups, tents okay, reservations (509) 773-3111, wheelchair access, pets okay, shower, pool, trailer waste disp., $16/night.

Located in Goldendale, at 821 Simcoe Dr.

T) MARYHILL STATE PARK

50 sites w/full hookups, community kitchen, wheelchair access, trailer waste disp., on river, boat launch, fishing, swimming, wind surfing, water skiing, $10 to $16/night.

Take State Hwy. 14 east of it junction with US Hwy. 97 for 2 miles to this state park.

U) COLUMBIA HILLS RV PARK

35 sites w/full hookups, tents okay, reservations (509) 767-2277, pets okay, showers, laundry, store, propane, $5 to $18/night.

Located 1.5 miles north of The Dalles Bridge at 111 Hwy. 197.

U) HORSETHIEF LAKE STATE PARK

12 units, some trailers - no hookups, trailer waste disposal, boat launches to Columbia River & Horsethief Lake, scuba diving area, fishing, pets okay, $10/night.

Take State Hwy. 14 west of its junction with US Hwy. 97 for 18 miles.

V) MOSS CREEK FS CAMP

17 single family sites - 10 reservable mid-May to mid-Sept. - (800) 280-CAMP, trailers to 32, piped water, on river, wheelchair access, fishing, in Gifford Pinchot NF, $9/night, elev. 1400'.

Located north of Cook 8 miles on County Road 18.

W) OKLAHOMA FS CAMP

23 single family sites - 14 reservable mid-May to mid-Sept. call (800) 280-CAMP, trailers to 22', well, on Little White Salmon River, wheelchair access, fishing, in Gifford Pinchot NF, $6/night, elev. 1700'.

Located north of Cook 14.4 miles on County Road 18.

X) HOME VALLEY PARK

23 units, tents okay, showers, picnic area, wheelchair access, information (509) 427-9478, pets okay, on Columbia River, swimming, fishing, windsurfing, $12/night - $7 for county residents.

Located just east of Carson, on State Hwy. 14.

X) HOME VALLEY GROCERY/RV

5 sites w/water & elec. plus grassy tent area, reservations (509) 427-5300, pit toilets, groceries, $3 to $8/night.

Located in Carson.

X) BIG FOOT TRAILER PARK

19 campsites w/full hookups, tents okay, reservations (509) 427-4411, trailer waste disposal, $5 to $10/night.

Located in Carson, at 1861 Metzger Rd.

Y) CARSON HOT SPRINGS

12 RV campsites w/full hookups, tents okay, reservations (509) 427-8292, showers, mineral water bathhouses, massage, picnic area, handicap access, trailer waste disposal, fishing, hiking, golf course, $4.50 to $12.50/night.

Located in Carson. At the flashing yellow light go up the hill, past the 4way stop and golf course. Take an immediate left and go down the hill to the resort.

Z) PANTHER CREEK FS CAMP

33 units - 25 single family sites plus 8 multi-family sites - 20 & 6 reservable mid-May thru Labor Day, (800) 280-CAMP, trailers to 25', well, stream, fishing, hiking - bridge to Pacific Crest Trail, big trees, horse trails & ramp, in Gifford Pinchot NF, $9 to $18/night.

Take County Road 92135 northwest of Carson 9 miles, then follow FSR 6517 east 1.5 miles and FSR 65 south .1 mile to camp.

AA) PARADISE CREEK FS CAMP

42 units - 34 single family sites & 8 multi-family sites - 27 & 4 reservable mid-May thru mid-Sept., (800) 280-CAMP, trailers to 25' - easy RV parking, well, located next to river, wheelchair access, fishing, hiking, in Gifford Pinchot NF, $9 to $16/night, elev. 1500'.

Take County Road 92135 northwest of Carson 13.8 miles, then follow FSR 30 north 6.3 miles.

BB) BEAVER FS CAMP

24 units - 19 single family sites & 5 multi-family sites - 15 & 4 reservable mid-May thru mid-Sept., (800) 280-CAMP, paved sites - trailers to 25', flush toilets, wheelchair access, horseshoe pits, game area, next to Wind River, swimming, hiking, fishing, near Trapper Creek Wilderness Area, in Gifford Pinchot NF, $9 to $18/night, elev. 1100'.

Located northwest of Carson 12.2 miles on County Road 30.

CC) BEACON ROCK STATE PARK

33 campsites, community kitchen shelter, wheelchair access, trailer waste disposal, on river, boat launch, fishing, trail to the top of Beacon Rock, pets okay, $10/night.

Located west of North Bonneville, about 6 miles, on State Hwy. 14.

Vacation #8

Exploring Washington's Olympic Peninsula

The serene waters of Lake Quinault provide a peaceful setting for getting in touch with nature. Carved by glaciers, its waters are deep and clear.

FROM THE AUTHOR'S JOURNAL · · ·

I can still remember the first time I camped at Lake Quinault. The setting sun turned the water into a bright orange pool, and as it disappeared, darkness dropped like a hood, leaving nothing beyond the circle of the campfire. Wild critters scurried, hooted, howled, and created a night-long symphony of sounds.

On this trip I find that campsites along the lake fill up by noon, where the setting is more like a well-worn carpet than a forest and the night sounds are loud and human made.

Although a visit to Lake Quinault is an important part of seeing the peninsula, one must now head way off the beaten track in order to find solitude. Backpackers must hike further, and those travelling by car need to drive a much greater distance.

During this recent visit, after one night at the lake, I drove nearly 25 miles to an isolated campground, along a network of gravel roads that took me past a couple of nice hiking/horse trails. The campground was filled with old-growth trees, each so large that it would take three adults with fully outstretched arms to circle its girth. Although my stay was in mid-August, only one other family occupied this rambling creek-side camp.

Considering the peninsula's proximity to Seattle, I was thrilled to still find something so wild.

Reflections on a quarter century of camping on the Olympic Peninsula

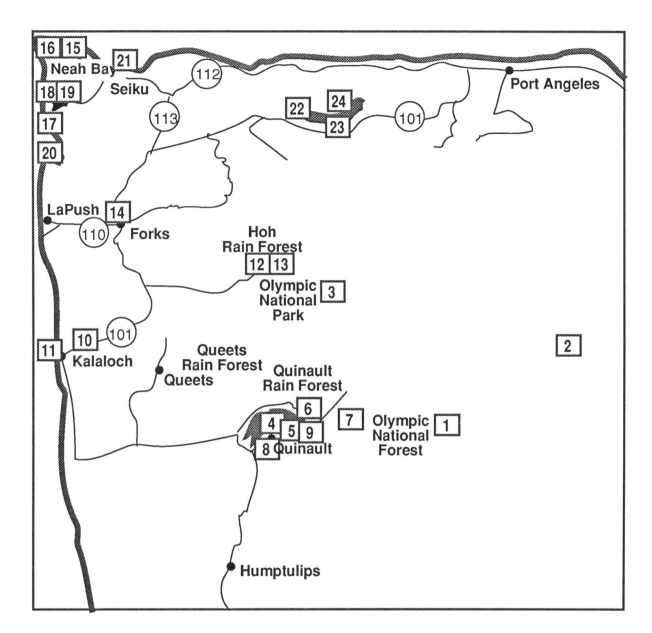

Olympic Peninsula Attractions

The Olympic Peninsula holds America's last wilderness beach and rain forest, plus large stands of moss-hung old-growth trees. Even though the eastern side of the peninsula is also special, this vacation focuses primarily on the western side.

The 632,000 acre **Olympic National Forest [1]** includes 5 wilderness areas, 200 miles of trails and 44 lakes, plus 800 miles of rivers and streams. Pacific salmon, steelhead, cutthroat, eastern brook and rainbow trout are all caught in its waters.

Ask Forest Service personnel to help you pick a trail or fishing area right for your talents. Mountain bikers will enjoy the **Big Quilcene Trail [2]**, south of Quilcene.

The **Olympic National Park [3]** protects a beautiful 57-mile-long unspoiled beach area as well as North America's only temperate rain forests. Hikers will find over 600 miles of trails in this 922,000 acre park; dogs are not permitted on trails. There is a charge of $10 per car, or $5 per person, to enter the park.

Lake Quinault [4] is surrounded by forest. Carved by glaciers, the water is deep and clear. Take **Lake Quinault Loop Trail [5]** along the south shore for a close-up look. This 4 mile easy hike includes a boardwalk through a cedar swamp. Lake fishing requires a special permit.

The 25-mile **Quinault Valley Auto Tour [6]** can be driven in less than 2 hours, but you'll probably want to allow more time. It offers views of Lake Quinault and the Quinault River, plus access to **Colonel Bob Wilderness [7]**. It is not recommended for RVs and trailers.

The **Big Tree Grove [8]**, 2 miles east of US Hwy. 101, is a self-guided nature trail with signs explaining this area's natural history. You'll find the **World's largest spruce [9]** 1.5 miles east of Quinault, and one of the world's largest cedars, a few miles north of Kalaloch Camp. The **Big Cedar Tree [10]** is on the east side of US Hwy. 101.

The Kalaloch area also has several short **beach trails [11]**; each is different from the others. Tidepools, ruby red gemstone slivers, beachcombing, ocean fishing and clamming are all great reasons for exploring every trail.

The **Hoh Rain Forest & Visitor Center [12]** is 19 miles east of US Hwy. 101 via a paved road. The rain forest is carpeted with moss, ferns, lichens and tiny plants, while overhead the light shimmers through a high canopy of clubmoss draped big leaf maples, giant douglas fir, sitka spruce, western red cedar and hemlock. Some are over 300 feet tall and 60 feet around. Roosevelt elk thrive on the forest's heavy undergrowth; 300 kinds of plants grow here.

The **Hall of Moss Trail [13]** is an easy loop covering less than a mile, Sprucc Nature Trail is just over a mile long, and there is a short, wheelchair accessible paved trail off the parking lot. Backpackers will enjoy the 18 mile trail that starts here, and ends at Mount Olympus, passing Elk Lake along the way. Permits are required for all overnight hikes.

The **Forks Timber Museum [14]** includes old logging photos and memorabilia, a real steam donkey, antique logging tools, and a fire lookout tower. The museum is free, and open mid-April thru October from 10:00 a.m. to 5:00 p.m. Tuesday thru Saturday and 1:00 p.m. to 5:00 p.m. on Sundays. During November and December it is open Saturday and Sunday only. It is closed the rest of the year.

The **Makah Indian Museum [15]** at Neah Bay provides an opportunity to learn about a group of people that has lived here since about 1000 BC. It showcases thousands of artifacts, including a variety of carved canoes, sea lion buoys made by the tribe's early whalers, and a recreated life-size longhouse. The latter provides a walk-thru look at how the tribe once lived. The museum is open daily during the summer, 10:00 a.m. to

5:00 p.m., and Wednesday thru Sunday the rest of the year. The cost is $5.00, and they have a wonderful shop that sells Indian-made items.

The **Cape Flattery Trail [16]** at Neah Bay will take you to the western-most point in the continental United States. A one hour round trip hike, it provides views of Tatoosh Island, Hole-in-the-Wall, Vancouver Island and the Pacific Coastline.

At the end of Lake Ozette Road, southwest of Sekiu, you will find two 4 mile trails. One takes you to the ocean, past a number of **Indian petroglyphs [17]**, the other to an ancient Indian village site and **Cape Alva [18]**. This site has been occupied for over 2,000 years.

The **Ozette Archaeological Site [19]** was revealed in 1970, and included three houses buried by a mudflow 500 years ago. Over 50,000 artifacts were found, including cedar-bark pouches, whaling harpoon blades, looms, spindle whorls, pendants, hats, toys, and ceremonial items. Many are on display at the Makah Museum.

The **Cape Trail [20]** will take you south 18 miles to Rialto Beach and LaPush, along the National Park's wilderness beach. Spring hikers might see whales migrating north.

The **Hoko Archaeological Site [21]**, near the mouth of the Hoko River, marks a 2,500-year-old fishing camp. Cedar handled knives with thumbnail-size quartz blades, wooden fishhooks, a fishing net, harpoon tips, the remains of a canoe dragway and drying racks were unearthed here. The Makah Museum also has many of the Hoko artifacts on display.

Lake Crescent [22] is glacier carved, 8.5 miles long, and 600 feet deep. Waterskiing, fishing, and paddlewheel boat tours are popular. The tours operate 4 to 5 times a day, from late May to October, take about 75 minutes, and cost $15.00.

You can drive around the lake's south shore, and will find a short trail near the ranger station leading to 90' **Marymere Falls [23]**. Hikers and mountain bikers can explore the north shore on the 8-mile-long **Spruce Railroad Trail [24]**.

For Additional Information

If you will be visiting the Olympic Peninsula, you may want to call the following numbers for further information.

Olympic National Park
(360) 452-4501

Olympic National Forest
(360) 956-2300

Quinault Ranger District
(360) 288-2525

Soleduck Ranger District
(360) 374-6522

Makah Indian Museum
(360) 645-2711

Forks Chamber of Commerce
(360) 374-2531

Olympic Peninsula Accommodations

ABERDEEN

Aberdeen Mansion Inn B&B
(888) 533-7079 or (360) 533-7079
807 N "M" St.
5 rooms, private baths, no smoking,
$95-125, includes full breakfast.

Lytle House B&B (800) 677-2320
509 Chenault Ave. (360) 533-2320
8 rooms in historic house, pri. baths,
kitchenettes, $65-135, inc. breakfast.

Nordic Inn Motel (360) 533-0100
1700 S Boone St. - South Aberdeen
66 rooms, pets okay, disabled access,
restaurant, $40-70.

Red Lion Inn (360)532-5210
521 W Wishkah
67 rooms, pets okay, disabled access,
downtown, $84-94, includes continen-
tal breakfast.

Thunderbird Motel (360) 532-3153
410 W Wishkah
36 rooms, pets okay, disabled access,
hot tub/spa, downtown, $50-64.

Towne Motel (360) 533-2340
712 Wishkah
24 rooms, pets okay, $30-55.

Travel-Lure Motel (360) 532-3280
623 W Wishkah
24 rooms, pets okay, disabled access,
downtown, $35-60.

FORKS

Bagby's Town Motel (800) 742-2429
1080 S Forks Ave. (360) 374-6231
20 units - 3 cabins, kitchenettes, disabled access, pets okay, BBQ area,
exercise room, $46-75 ($34-40).

Forks Motel (360) 374-6243
351 Forks Ave. S
73 rooms, kitchens & jacuzzi suite,
dis. access, pets okay, pool, $47-70.

Huckleberry Lodge B&B
(888) 822-6008 or (360) 374-6008
1171 Big Pine Way
5 rooms - 2 cabins, private baths, on
Calawah River, no pets, hot tub, game
room, $75-95, includes full breakfast.

Manitou Lodge B&B (360) 374-6295
Kilmer Rd. off Mora Rd.
6 rooms/cabins, private baths, kids
okay, disabled access, pets - $10 fee,
exercise room, $70-90, includes full
breakfast.

Miller Tree Inn (360) 374-6806
654 E Division St.
7 rooms, private baths, no smoking,
pets - $10 fee, hot tub, $60-90,
includes breakfast.

Olympic Suites (800) 262-3433
800 Olympic Dr.
28 1-2 bedroom suites w/kitchen &
living room, no pets, $75-85 ($60-70).

Rain Forest Hostel (360) 374-2270
169312 US Hwy. 101 S
(23 miles south of Forks)
12 bunk & family rooms, showers,
shared kitchen & library, on bus line,
$10/bed.

Shady Nook Cottage B&B
81 Ash Ave. (360) 374-5497
2 cottages w/kitchens, no smoking, no
pets, no kids under 12, near downtown, picnic area, $65-75, no credit
cards.

HOQUIAM

Sandstone Motel (360) 533-6383
2424 Aberdeen Ave.
24 rooms, pets okay, $35-65.

Snore & Whisker Motel
3031 Simpson Ave. (360) 532-5060
11 units - some w/kitchenettes & in-
room jacuzzi, handicap access, pets
okay, $35 and up.

Westwood Inn (800) 562-0992
910 Simpson Ave. (360) 532-8161
65 units, disabled access, pets okay, kitchenettes, downtown, $45-150.

Y Motel (360) 532-5265
408 US Hwy. 101 North
15 rooms, pets okay, $40-80, includes continental breakfast.

KALALOCH

Kalaloch Lodge (360) 962-2271
157151 US Hwy. 101
60 units, cabins w/kitchenettes & fireplaces, in Olympic National Park, overlooks ocean, pets okay, disabled access, restaurant, $55-187.

NEAH BAY

The Cape Motel & RV Park
Bayview Ave. (360) 645-2250
10 units - 5 cabins, kitchens, laundry, pets okay, also 50 RV sites w/hookups & tent spaces, showers, trailer waste disposal, near museum, $45-64.

Tyee Motel (360) 645-2223
42 rooms, pets okay, also RV sites w/hookups, showers, trailer waste disposal, $35-95.

PORT ANGELES AREA
(West of town)

Lake Crescent Lodge
416 Lake Crescent Rd. (360) 928-3211
53 rooms in historic lodge, on Lake Crescent, wheelchair access, pets okay, restaurant, rowboat rentals, $72-153.

Log Cabin Resort (360) 327-3583
3183 East Beach Rd. - Lake Crescent
20 rooms & 8 cabins, on Lake Crescent, pets okay, laundry, also 40 RV sites w/hookups, $47-118.

Sol Duc Hot Springs Resort
Sol Duc River Rd. (360) 327-3583
32 cabins - 6 have kitchens - each sleeps 2-4 people, plus 20 RV sites w/hookups for water & electricity, situated in Olympic National Forest, pets okay, 3 hot mineral pools, massage therapist, freshwater swimming pool, restaurant, grocery store, hiking trails, only open from mid-May thru mid-Sept., cabins: 2 people $87-97 plus $12.50 per additional person, RV sites $16.00.

QUINAULT

Lake Quinault Lodge (800) 562-6672
345 S Shore Rd. (360) 288-2900
92 units in historic lakeside lodge, fireplace & pet rooms available, indoor pool & spa, restaurant & lounge, outdoor lawn area for games & relaxation, on Lake Quinault, $62-140.

Lake Quinault Resort Motel
314 N Shore Rd. (800) 650-2362
9 units - some suites & kitchenettes, view of Lake Quinault, quiet setting, handicap access, no pets or smoking, nightly campfires on beach, $99-119 ($50-70).

SEKIU

Bay Motel (360) 963-2444
15562 State Hwy. 112
16 units - some w/kitchens, kids welcome, pets okay, popular with those who fish, $50-70.

Herb's Motel (360) 963-2346
411 Front St.
12 view rooms - some w/kitchen, pets only w/prior approval - $10 fee, BBQ area, $40-85.

Olympic Peninsula Campgrounds & RV Parks

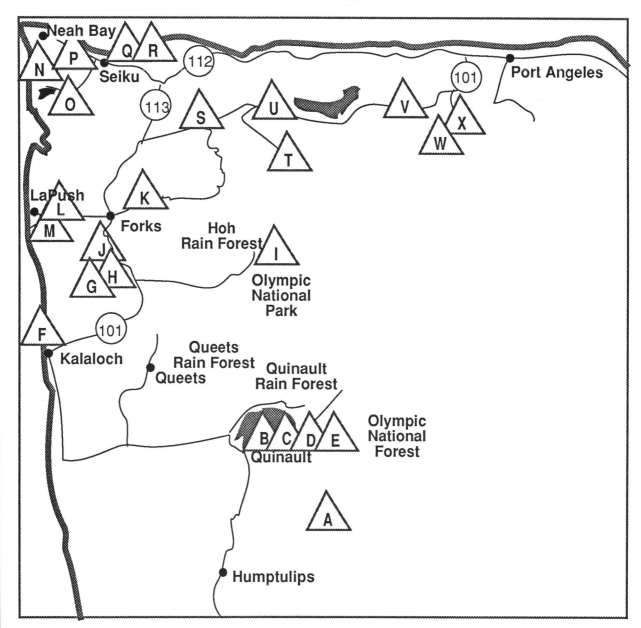

A) CAMPBELL TREE GROVE FS CAMP

11 units, trailers to 16', pit toilets, pump, creek, hiking trail, old growth trees, primitive, elev. 1100', no fee.

Follow US Hwy. 101 northeast of Humptulips 4 miles to Newbury Creek Rd. and head east 8 miles to FSR 2280. Follow this road for 11 miles.

B) FALLS CREEK FS CAMP

31 campsites, trailers to 16', flush toilets, wheelchair access, located on Lake Quinault, boat ramp, picnic shelter, swimming, fishing, hiking, $7 to $13/night.

Take South Shore Rd. northeast of Quinault for about .2 mile.

C) GATTON CREEK FS CAMP

5 tent sites, on lake, pit toilets, swimming, fishing, $7/night.

Take South Shore Rd. northeast of Quinault .5 mile.

D) WILLABY FS CAMP

22 units, trailers to 16', flush toilets, on lake, boat ramp, swimming, fishing, hiking, $13/night.

Take South Shore Rd. northeast of Quinault .5 mile.

E) RAIN FOREST RESORT VILLAGE & RV PARK

31 units w/hookups for water & elec., no tents, information (360) 288-2535, trailers to 38', showers, laundry, groceries, restaurant, on Lake Quinault, swimming, fishing, hiking, canoe rental, pets okay, open year round, $16/night

Take South Shore Rd. northeast of Quinault 1.5 miles.

F) KALALOCH NP CAMP

175 units plus small group site - group reservations (360) 962-2283, trailers to 21', handicap access, trailer waste disposal, ocean, fishing, hiking, year round, elev. 50', $12/night - group site $20 plus $1/person.

Located north of Queets 6 miles on US Hwy. 101.

G) HOH RIVER RESORT & RV PARK

24 units - 20 w/full hookups plus 4 w/water & elec., grassy tent area, reservations (360) 374-5566, showers, laundry, groceries, propane, trail to river, fishing, hiking, pets okay, $15/night.

Located on US Hwy. 101 about 15 miles south of Forks, at 175443 US Hwy. 101.

H) HARD RAIN CAFE & RV PARK

13 sites w/full hookups plus tent spaces, (360) 374-9288, pets welcome, disabled access, trailer waste disposal, $13-15.

Leave US Hwy. 101 south of Forks near the Hoh bridge on Upper Hoh Rd. Located at 5763 Upper Hoh Rd.

I) HOH RIVER NP CAMP

89 units, trailers to 21', handicap access, trailer waste disposal, river, fishing, hiking, year round, elev. 578', $10/night.

About 14 miles south of Forks via US Hwy. 101 and east on Hoh River Rd. 19 miles.

J) BOGACHIEL STATE PARK

42 units - 6 w/hookups for water & elec. plus 34 standard & 2 primitive sites, trailers to 35', flush toilets, showers, community kitchen, picnic area, trailer waste disposal, on Bogachiel River, fishing, open year round, $7 to $16/night.

To get there, follow US Hwy. 101 south of Forks 6 miles.

J) 101 RV PARK

40 sites w/full hookups plus tent spaces, (360) 374-5073, showers, in town, $16 to $24/night.

Located at 901 S. Forks Ave. (101).

K) KLAHANIE FS CAMP

15 primitive tent sites, pit toilets, in rain forest, river, fishing, elev. 300', no fee.

Take US Hwy. 101 north of Forks 1.7 miles, and take FSR 29 east 5.4 miles to campground.

L) MORA NP CAMPGROUND

94 campsites plus walk-in small group site, group reservations (360) 374-5460, trailers to 21', handicap access, trailer waste disposal, ocean access, on Quinault River, swimming, fishing, hiking, open year round, $10/night - group site $20/night plus $1/person.

Located in La Push.

M) LA PUSH OCEAN PARK RESORT

55 units w/hookups for water & elec., no tents, reservations (800) 487-1267, trailers to 50', showers, laundry, wheelchair access, fishing, hiking, pets okay, open year round, $15/night.

Located in La Push.

N) HOBUCK BEACH PARK

28 campsites, tents okay, cabins w/kitchens - 2 night min., reservations

(360) 645-2422, trailers to 30', no pets in cabins, on bay, fishing, hiking, $10/night - cabins $50.

Located 3 miles southwest of Neah Bay.

O) OZETTE NP CAMP

15 tent units, walk-in, hiking, beach access, elev. 80', $10/night.

Located at Ozette Lake, follow the road out of Sekiu.

P) TRETTEVIKS RV PARK

29 RV sites w/hookups plus 20 tent spaces, on Strait of Juan de Fuca, pets okay, sandy beach, beach fires, fishing, $13 to $17/night.

Take State Hwy. 112 west of Sekiu 8 miles to 6850 State Hwy. 112.

Q) OLSON'S RESORT

190 units - 50 w/water/elec./sewer, 10 w/elec., plus 90 w/out hookups, tents okay, plus 27 cabins - some w/kitchen, reservations, (360) 963-2311, trailers to 40', showers, laundry, wheelchair access, groceries, fishing, boat launch/rental & gas, open year round, campsites $12/night.

Located in Sekiu, at 440 Front St.

R) CURLEY'S RESORT

RV & tent sites - 10 w/hookups, reservations (800) 542-9680, scuba diving tours & dive shop, on Strait of Juan de Fuca, pets okay - $10 fee, espresso & ice cream bar, boat moorage, bbq area, $15/night.

Located at the east end of Sekiu.

S) KLAHOWYA NF CAMP

55 units, trailers to 30', reservations (800) 280-2267, flush toilets, handicap access, river, ramp, fishing, hiking, $12/night.

Take US Hwy. 101 west of Port Angeles 40 miles to milepost #212 and campground.

T) SOLEDUCK NP CAMP

80 campsites plus group area, trailers to 21', handicap access, trailer waste disposal, on Soleduck River, swimming, fishing, hiking, elev. 1680', $12/night - groups $20/night plus $1/person.

Take US Hwy. 101 west of Port Angeles 28 miles and follow the Soleduck River Rd. southeast 12 miles to the campground.

U) FAIRHOLM NP CAMPGROUND

87 units, trailers to 21', handicap access, trailer waste disposal, on Lake Crescent, swimming, fishing, boat launch & rental, hiking, open year round, elev. 580', $10/night.

To get to Fairholm, take US Hwy. 101 west of Port Angeles about 26 miles and watch for sign.

V) SHADOW MOUNTAIN

60 units - 40 w/hookups for water/elec./sewer plus 20 tent sites, reservations (360) 928-3043, trailers to 70', showers, laundry, wheelchair access, playground, store, propane, gas, trailer waste disposal, at Lake Crescent, boat launch, swimming, fishing, hiking, pets okay, open year round, $13 to $19/night.

Shadow Mountain is located along US Hwy. 101 about 15 miles west of Port Angeles.

W) ALTAIRE NP CAMP

30 campsites, trailers to 21', handicap accessible restrooms, on Elwha River, elev. 450', open June thru Sept., $10/night.

At about 7 miles west of Port Angeles, along US Hwy. 101, follow the Olympic Hot Springs Road south for about 5 miles to Altaire.

X) ELWHA NP CAMP

41 campsites, trailers to 21', handicap accessible restrooms, on Elwha River, hiking, elev. 390', open year round, $10/night.

To get to Elwha, follow US Hwy. 101 7 miles west of Port Angeles and take the Olympic Hot Springs Road south 3 miles.

Vacation #9

Alpine Adventures
in the Wallowa Mountains

The Wallowa Mountains are some of the tallest in the Northwest, with a dozen over 8,000 feet tall. The scenery is gorgeous, and the landscape deserving of its nickname of *America's Swiss Alps*.

FROM THE AUTHOR'S JOURNAL . . .

The first time I stood on the summit of Mt. Howard, 8,200 feet above sea level, I was much too young to be impressed by the view. Instead I was thrilled by the excitement of riding a tramway up the side of a mountain, exploring its alpine trails, and feeding the nearly-tame ground squirrels.

As I've matured, each return visit has left me more impressed with that expansive view. It's the best, and easiest place to go for a birdseye look at Wallowa Lake's splendor, a panorama that includes over a dozen mile-and-a-half tall mountains, and a crisp alpine setting where glaciers never melt.

When I visit the Wallowas it's now a tradition for me to begin with a trip up Mt. Howard. Once there I sit in the sun, looking over the surrounding mountains with maps of local trails, and select the one I will later hike. Then, as I hike the trail, I can visualize my location by calling to mind that earlier view.

It's not hard to understand why the Nez Perce Indians found this region so important. As impressive as the landscape is now, I can only begin to imagine what it was like when they alone walked its lands.

This corner of Oregon has so much beauty to offer the visitor. Perhaps its harsh winters and isolation will help to insure that it stays that way!

Notes from my most recent visit to the top of Mt. Howard, in the Wallowa Mountains

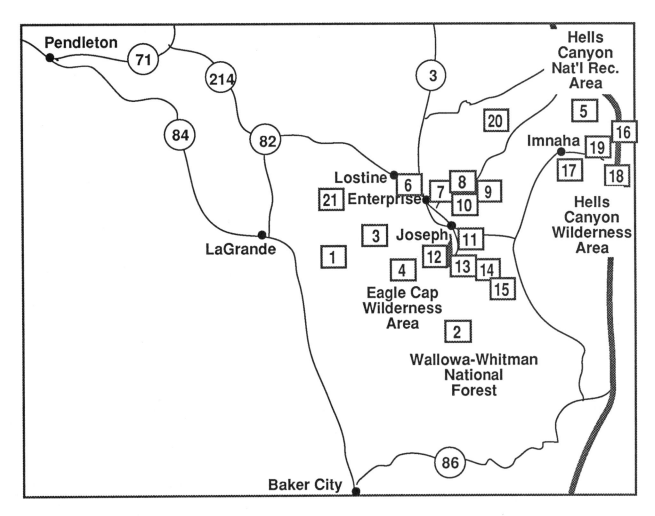

Wallowa Mountain Area Attractions

Oregon's northeast corner is where you'll find the state's tallest mountains. The **Wallowa Mountains [1]** are said to resemble the Swiss Alps, and include at least 12 peaks over 8,000 feet. The tallest, **Matterhorn [2]**, is 9,845 feet.

Hikers, backpackers, and those who enjoy travelling by horse will love the variety of trails. They range from easy day hikes to strenuous mountain treks that take weeks to cover.

In total, there are hundreds of miles of trails within the **Wallowa-Whitman National Forest [3]**. The 358,000 acre **Eagle Cap Wilderness Area [4]** alone has 500 miles of trails, and the Oregon portion of the **Hells Canyon National Recreation Area [5]** an additional 900 miles.

Visitors will want to stop at the **Forest Service Center [6]**, located west of Enterprise. As headquarters for the Hells Canyon National Recreation Area, Eagle Cap Wilderness and the Wallowa Valley Ranger District, it's a one-stop source for information on local trails, scenery, wildlife, geology, history and Indian lore.

Birdwatchers will want to ask about the rare Wallowa gray-crowned rose finch that nests only in the Wallowas.

Exhibits explain the region's life zones, provide details on the area's Native Americans, include local photographs, a scaled relief map of Wallowa County, discovery drawers, and audio tapes.

This has been the ancestral home of the Nez Perce Indians for over 120 centuries. Carvings, rock faces, paintings, and the remains of their camps exist throughout the area. In order to avoid forced relocation this peaceful tribe fled their homeland in 1877.

They were captured near Canada, after a 1700 mile flight, and confined to a reservation in eastern Washington. Each July the town of Joseph honors this bit of history with **Chief Joseph Days [7]**.

You can learn about area settlers, Chief Joseph, the Nez Perce Indians, and that famous flight to Canada at the **Wallowa County Museum [8]** in Joseph. It is open daily from mid-May through September.

Be sure to ask when the next **1896 Bank Robbery and Gunfight Re-enactment [9]** will happen on Main Street. Art lovers will also want to tour the town's many **art galleries [10]**.

Just south of Joseph you'll see a **National Indian Cemetery [11]**. It has long served as a burial place for Nez Perce and Umatilla Indians.

Wallowa Lake [12], 10 miles south of Enterprise, was created by glaciers about a million years ago. It is 283 feet deep, and a classic morraine-held glacial lake.

Fishing for giant Makinaw, trout and kokanee, as well as swimming and boating, are popular. Paddleboats, rowboats and motorboats can all be rented at the lake. Anglers may also want to try one of the region's numerous alpine lakes.

Wallowa Lake State Park [13], at the head of the lake, is always a busy place. Campers without reservations will most likely have to look for an overnight site elsewhere, but anyone can make use of the park's day-use facilities.

The best way to view Wallowa Lake is from the **Wallowa Lake Tramway [14]**, which is east of the lake's southern end. It provides an exciting way to reach the top of 8,200 foot **Mt. Howard [15]**. You can get out at the top and spend as much time as you like exploring during operating hours. The trip takes about 20 minutes each way.

This is the steepest tramway of its kind in North America, and provides some terrific views. You're securely encased, and glide along at an average height of 30 feet above the ground.

At the top, you'll find several miles of easy trails, and a view of four states. The tramway operates from the weekend before Memorial Day until the third week of September. The cost is about $10.00 per person, and half fare for young children. A bargain at any price, it provides an excellent way to see the countryside without expending a lot of energy.

Another way to get an aerial view of the mountains is by taking a scenic flight out of the airport at Joseph. These include passes over **Hells Canyon [16]**, North America's deepest river gorge, which separates Oregon and Idaho.

Until recently, flying was the only way to get a good view of the canyon, unless you were willing to hike for miles, or had access to a rugged vehicle.

Today, anyone can get a close look at the canyon via the **Wallowa Valley Loop Road [17]**, southeast of Joseph. This 54 mile route follows paved roads; views include the **Snake River [18]** and **Hat Point [19]**. Hat Point towers nearly 8,000 feet above the canyon floor.

The **Chesnimnus-Buckhorn Loop [20]**, is another great day-long adventure. You can follow this route into the historic Wallowa high sheep country, past elk meadows, the Imnaha and Snake River canyons, to Buckhorn and Red Hill Lookouts, and Billy Meadows Station. The loop begins south of Enterprise on Zumwalt Road, and travels over Forest Service Road #46, Elk Creek Road, and Highway 3.

Camera buffs and backpackers will also enjoy the **Lostine River Canyon Area [21]**. To get there, take Highway 82 north of Enterprise to the town of Lostine and follow Lostine River Road south. You'll soon find yourself in a beautiful wilderness area, travelling along a river that drops at a startling rate. Gorgeous scenery, hiking trails, and mountain lakes are all found here.

Wallowa County is host to a number of annual events and festivals. These include the Wallowa Mountain High Hot Air Balloon Festival in mid-June, Jazz at the Lake and Chief Joseph Days in July, and the Hells Canyon Mule Days and Alpenfest in September.

All make excellent times for a family vacation. You can get complete information on these, and other local happenings, by calling the Wallowa County Chamber of Commerce.

Although July and August are the most popular times to visit this area, the well prepared visitor can camp any time between May and October.

For Additional Information

If you plan on visiting this area, and would like additional information, call any of the following:

Wallowa Mountains Visitor Center
(541) 426-4978

Wallowa County Chamber of Commerce
(800) 585-4121

Joseph Chamber of Commerce
(541) 432-1015

Wallowa Lake State Park
(541) 432-4185

Wallowa Lake Tramway
(541) 432-5331

Wallowa Mountains Area Accommodations

ENTERPRISE

Best Western Rama Inn
(541) 426-2000
1200 Highland Ave.
53 rooms w/ref. & micro., some view rooms, indoor pool, hot tub & sauna, no pets, open year round, $80-140.

Country Inn
(541) 426-4986
402 W North St.
11 rooms plus 3 suites, all rooms inc. ref. - some have microwaves, suites have full kitchens, no pets, open year round, $42-70.

George Hyatt House B&B
(800) 95-Hyatt or (541) 426-0241
200 E Greenwood
4 rooms w/private baths in lovely 1898 Queen Anne Victorian-style home, hot tub, no smoking, no pets, $95 per couple, includes breakfast.

Lozier's Country Loft B&B
(888) 323-3271 or (541) 426-3271
81922 Fish Hatchery Lane
2 room suite w/private bath, cathedral ceilings & mountain view, popular w/birders, hot air balloon, no pets, no credit cards, year round, $89-119.

Perkins House B&B
(541) 426-3938
107 W. Second St.
1 & 2 bedroom suites w/private baths, kitchens & sitting rooms, some pets okay, no credit cards, open year round, $65-85.

Ponderosa Motel (541) 426-3186
102 SE Greenwood
25 rooms w/microwave & ref., pets okay - $5 fee, walk to restaurants & shops, open year round, $52-74.

Tickled Trout Inn
(541) 426-6039
507 S River St.
3 rooms, no pets, no credit cards, $65-85/night.

Wilderness Inn
(541) 426-4535 or (800) 965-1205
301 W North St.
28 rooms plus 1 suite w/hot tub & kitchen, sauna, pets okay - $5 fee, open year round, $52-123.

JOSEPH

Chandlers' Bed, Bread & Trail Inn
(800) 452-3781 or (541) 432-9675
700 S Main
5 rooms - 3 w/private bath in farm-style setting @ foot of Wallowas, inc. country breakfast, sun room, streamside gazebo, kitchen, no pets, $60-80.

Dragon Meadows B&B
(541) 432-1027
504 N Lake St.
2 rooms w/shared bath, no pets, open year round, $65/couple, inc. breakfast.

Indian Lodge Motel
(541) 432-2651
201 S Main
16 rooms - some w/refrigerator, pets okay - $10 fee, can walk to restaurants, open year round, $36-57.

Mountain View Motel
(541) 432-2982
83450 Joseph Hwy.
9 rooms - some w/kitchenettes, located in a country setting w/mountain view, pets okay - $5 fee, open year round, $44-61.

Wallowa River Camp

(888) WRiverC or (541) 432-9043
501 Park Dr.
Bed & breakfast rooms, hostel-style bunkhouse & cedar-floored tepees, some kitchen units, horse area, no pets allowed, located along Wallowa River, call for rates.

HALFWAY

Clear Creek Farms B&B

(541) 742-2238
48212 Clear Creek Rd.
4 rooms in farmhouse w/private bath plus 1 rustic and 1 open-air cabin, kids welcome, pets okay, hot tub by prior arrangement, working farm w/bison herd, horse facilities available, stocked fishing pond, $60-66, inc. farm breakfast.

Pine Valley Lodge

(541) 742-2027
Located in downtown Halfway
Eclectic group of historic buildings offering rooms - some w/shared bath plus bunkhouse & 4 bedroom home, $55 and up, some include kitchen facilities, comfortable shared great room, mannered pets okay, fine dining nearby.

OXBOW

Hells Canyon B&B

(541) 785-3373
Homestead Road
Simple rooms w/private bath, overlooks Hells Canyon, walk to Snake River, open year round, no smoking, $50 per couple, includes continental breakfast.

WALLOWA LAKE

Eagle Cap Chalets

(541) 432-4704
59879 Wallowa Lake Hwy.
37 rooms plus suites, condos & cabins, some kitchen units, handicap access rooms, indoor pool & hot tub, no pets, open year round, $48-100.

Flying Arrow Resort

(541) 432-2951
59782 Wallowa Lake Hwy.
21 1-4 bedroom fully equipped cabins, kitchen units, fireplaces, sun decks, pool, hot tub, no pets, at confluence of East Fork & Wallowa Rivers, $63-170.

Matterhorn Swiss Village

(541) 432-4071
59950 Wallowa Lake Hwy.
9 cabins w/kitchens, no pets, $50-85.

Ram's Head Cottage

(541) 432-2002
84591 Pine Ridge Rd.
2 units, kitchen units, no pets, no credit cards, $115-160.

Stein's Cabins

(541) 432-2391
84681 Ponderosa Lane
11 cabins, kitchen units, pets okay, $55-85.

Tamarack Pines B&B Inn

(541) 432-2920
60073 Wallowa Lake Hwy.
4 rooms, hot tub, no pets, $40-60.

Wallowa Lake Lodge

(541) 432-9821
60060 Wallowa Lake Hwy.
28 rooms & 8 cabins, restaurant, no pets, $70-175.

Wallowa Mountain Area Campgrounds & RV Parks

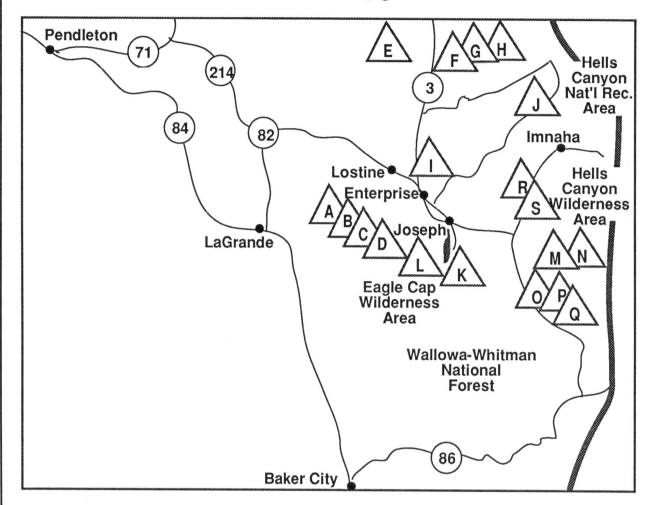

A) WILLIAMSON FS CAMP

10 campsites, trailers to 18', no drinking water available, on river, swimming, fishing, trailheads to wilderness area, elev. 5000', no fee.

Head south of Lostine for 7 miles on CR 551 and follow the gravel road (FSR 8210) south for 4 miles to the campground.

B) RIVERQUEST HORSE ADVENTURE RANCH

Bed & barn accommodations for horse enthusiasts, dorm-style accommodations, hot tub, showers, corrals, meals available, on 45 acres in the Wallowa Mountains. Call for rates - (541) 569-2493.

Located near the town of Lostine, at 78365 Caudle Lane.

C) SHADY FS CAMP

12 campsites, trailers to 18', no drinking water available, on river, swimming, fishing, wilderness area trailheads, elev. 5400', no fee.

Head south of Lostine for 7 miles on CR 551 and follow the gravel road (FSR 8210) south 10 miles to the campground.

D) TWO PAN FS CAMP

9 sites, some trailers to 18', no drinking water, river, swimming, fishing, wilderness trailheads, elev. 5600', no fee.

Head south of Lostine 7 miles on CR 551 and follow gravel FSR 8210 south 10.8 miles to campground.

E) MUD CREEK BLM REC. SITE

Scattered campsites, small boat ramp, on Grande Ronde River, information (541)523-4476, pets okay, no fee.

Follow State Highway 3 north of Enterprise 30 miles to Flora, go west 3 miles on Lost Prairie Road, northwest 3 miles on Troy Road, and head southwest 4 miles to campground.

F) VIGNE FS CAMP

7 units, trailers to 22', well, stream, fishing, primitive, elev. 3500', no fee.

Take State Hwy. 3 north of Enterprise 15 miles and go northeast 22 miles on FSR 46. The last 18 miles are gravel.

G) COYOTE FS CAMP

29 units, some trailers to 22', no drinking water, hiking, elev. 4800', no fee.

Follow State Hwy. 3 north of Enterprise 15 miles and FSR 46 northeast 30 miles. The last 26 miles are gravel.

H) DOUGHERTY SPRINGS FS CAMP

12 units, some trailers to 22', no drinking water, stream, elev. 5100', no fee.

Take State Hwy. 3 north of Enterprise for 15 miles and follow FSR 46 northeast 37 miles. The last 33 miles are gravel.

I) TROY WILDERNESS LODGE & RV PARK

20 RV sites w/elec. hookups, plus grassy tent area w/firepits, pets okay, reservation information (541) 426-4027, showers, gas, propane, elev. 3500', $5 to $9/night.

Go .5 mile north of Enterprise on State Hwy. 3.

I) OUTPOST RV PARK

48 RV sites w/water/elec./sewer, plus grassy tent area, pets okay, reservation information (541)426-4027, showers, elev. 3500', $10 to $17/night.

Located right in Enterprise, at 84570 Bartlett Road.

J) BUCKHORN FS CAMP

6 campsites, picnic area, no drinking water, spring, stock ramp, elev. 5200', no fee.

Take State Highway 82 south of Enterprise 3 miles, CR 772 northeast 5.2 miles, CR 798 northeast 25.8 miles, and FSR 46 northeast 9.6 miles to campground. The last 41 miles of travel are on gravel.

K) WALLOWA LAKE STATE PARK

210 units - 121 w/hookups for water/elec./sewer, 89 tent sites, plus 3 group tent areas & 2 yurts, reservations - (800) 551-6949, maximum site 90', showers, wheelchair access, picnic area, trailer waste disposal, boating, fishing, swimming, trails into Eagle Cap Wilderness, $11 to $20/night - group areas $60, yurts $27.

Follow Wallowa Lake Road south of Joseph 6 miles.

L) HURRICANE CREEK FS CAMP

8 units, some trailers to 18', picnic area, no drinking water, stream, fishing, trails into Eagle Cap Wilderness, primitive, elev. 4600', no fee.

Go 3.5 miles southwest of Joseph and take FSR 8205 south for .5 mile to the campground. This is a rough road, and is not recommended for RVs or low-clearance vehicles.

M) BLACKHORSE REC. AREA CAMP

16 units, trailers to 32', no drinking water, river, fishing, hiking, pets okay, elev. 4000', no fee.

Take State Hwy. 350 east of Joseph 7.7 miles and follow FSR 39 southeast 28.7 miles.

N) OLLOKOT REC. AREA CAMP

12 units, trailers to 32', no drinking water, river, fishing, pets okay, elev. 4000', no fee.

Take State Hwy. 350 east of Joseph 7.7 miles and follow FSR 39 southeast 28.8 miles to campground.

O) HIDDEN REC. AREA CAMP

13 units, some trailers to 32', no drinking water, river, fishing, hiking, pets okay, elev. 4400', no fee.

Take State Hwy. 350 east of Joseph 7.7 miles, FSR 39 southeast 28.8 miles, and FSR 3960 southwest 7 miles. This is a gravel road.

P) EVERGREEN FS CAMP

17 units, trailers to 32', no drinking water, primitive, river, swimming, fishing, hiking, in Hells Canyon National Recreation Area, elev. 4500', free.

Take State Hwy. 350 east of Joseph 7.7 miles, FSR 39 south 28.8 miles, and FSR 3960 southwest 8.0 miles. the last 8 miles are on a gravel road.

Q) INDIAN CROSSING REC. AREA CAMP

14 units, trailers to 32', no drinking water, river, fishing, horse ramp, pets okay, elev. 4500', no fee.

Take State Hwy. 350 east of Joseph 7.7 miles, FSR 39 southeast 28.8 miles, and gravel FSR 3960 southwest 8.8 miles.

R) SADDLE CREEK FS CAMP

6 units, trailers to 18', view, no drinking water, picnic area, hiking, elev. 6600', no fee.

Take FSR 4240 southeast of Imnaha 19.7 miles to campground. Steep road. Not recommended for RVs.

S) SACAJAWEA FS CAMP

3 tent units, picnic area, no drinking water, hiking, stock ramp, outstanding view, elev. 7000', free.

Head southeast of Imnaha 25 miles on FSR 4240, and follow FSR 315 east .7 mile to campground. Steep roads, not recommended for RVs.

Vacation #10

A Two Mountain Odyssey;
Mt. Saint Helens & Mt. Rainier

When Mt. St. Helens erupted in 1980 it made national news; by the time it settled down, it was over 1300 feet shorter than its earlier 9,677 feet.

FROM THE AUTHOR'S JOURNAL . . .

Growing up in Portland, my Mount St. Helens memories take two-distinctly different shapes. Prior to 1980 I used to hike there, in the shadow of a mountain resembling an ice cream cone that was just starting to soften, totally unaware that it might some day erupt.

Today, it's a mountain without a top, where you find forests thrown to the ground with such force that the trees look like a dropped box of toothpicks. The wildlife is just beginning to return, but its once crystal-clear lakes are still filled with ash.

The portion now called the Mount St. Helens National Volcanic Monument provides an unequalled opportunity to see what much of the Pacific Northwest landscape once looked like. Easily accessible to all, no one should leave this region without at least a brief tour.

On the other hand, Mount Rainier has changed little during my lifetime. It gained national park status in 1899, and has even managed to retain some of its old-growth areas. Although Rainier has more visitors than it did during my early visits, anyone willing to hike far enough will still find a natural experience.

Even if you aren't interested in hiking, you won't want to miss the viewpoints at Paradise and Sunrise. Between erupting volcanoes, and expanding populations, who knows what changes lie in this mountain's future.

Thoughts on a lifetime of changes to two of Washington's most beautiful mountains.

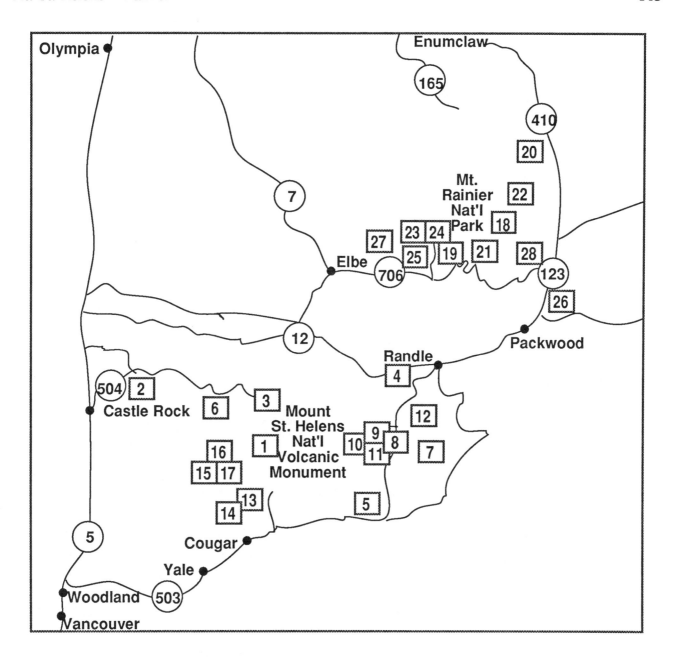

Mt. St. Helens & Rainier Area Attractions

On March 20, 1980 Mount St. Helens' first pre-eruption earthquake was reported. Seven days later the steam and ash eruptions began, continuing off and on until mid October.

Subsequent eruptions did not include ash, but added to the dome formation.

The former 9,677 foot mountain is now just 8,365 feet tall.

In 1982 the **Mount St. Helens National Volcanic Monument [1]** was established. Its **Visitor Center [2]**, 5 miles east of Castle Rock, is packed full of interesting exhibits on monument features and volcanic eruptions. Open year round, 9:00 a.m. to 6:00 p.m., it takes an hour or more to see all of the exhibits.

The **Coldwater Ridge Visitor Center [3]** and the new Mt. St. Helens Center are found on the mountain's northwest side; the information portals at **Woods Creek [4]** and **Pine Creek [5]**, to the northeast and southeast, are also good places to get current information on trails, weather conditions, road closures and attractions. The portals are staffed only during the summer season.

On the way to Coldwater Ridge be sure to stop at the **Toutle River Mudflow [6]**. Located at the edge of the blast area, this massive flow plugged the river valley, causing flooding and irreparable devastation.

As you travel around Mount St. Helens, you'll find lots of spots where you can get a good look at the mountain and destruction caused by its eruptions. To get really close to the mountain crater take **Loop Drive [7]**. It goes right up to the edge of the restricted zone, and takes you to some of the monument's best attractions.

At **Meta Lake [8]** you'll find a short paved trail and the remains of a car caught in the volcanic explosion. The **Independence Pass [9]** trail takes you along a ridge and provides a look into the crater. **Harmony Falls Trail [10]** is an easy one-mile path through a blown-down forest, past massive landslide areas, up to Spirit Lake's floating forest, and also provides great views of the lava dome and crater.

Windy Ridge [11], at the edge of the restricted zone, is just four miles from the crater and has a couple of real nice trails. If you have time, and a good vehicle, you may also want to take the road up **Strawberry Mountain [12]** for an aerial view of the dome and surrounding landscape.

Another good place to check out is **Ape Cave [13]**, on the south side of the mountain. After climbing down a short stairway you can explore either the easy lower or difficult upper cave. This 11,215 foot-long lava tube is the longest in North America and has been here for over 1900 years. You'll need two light sources, sturdy-soled shoes and a jacket. To get there follow FSR 90 and 83 about 10 miles from State Hwy. 503.

This is also the site of the **Trail of Two Forests [14]**, a short boardwalk through a 2,000 year-old lava cast forest. Signs explain how the tree molds were created, and some have ladders, so children can crawl through and explore.

If you follow FSR 83 an additional 7 miles to **Lahar Viewpoint [15]** you'll see the effects of a 60 mph eruption-caused mudflow. A short trail leads to a view of the volcano which is only 4 miles away at this point. From here you can explore **Lava Canyon [16]** or **Ape Canyon [17]**; the latter is a place where Bigfoot is said to have been spotted.

The lush beauty of **Mount Rainier [18]** is a complete contrast to the starkness of Mount St. Helens. This mountain has been a national park since 1899, and at 14,410 feet towers above surrounding forests. It too was created by a series of volcanic eruptions, none recent, which were followed by centuries of glacial erosion. Visitors will find crystal clear

The continent's longest lava tube cave is found on Mount St. Helens' southern side, and open for public exploration. It's a great place to spend a hot afternoon.

streams, old growth forests, cascading waterfalls, high mountain lakes and massive glaciers. The entry fee to this national park is $10 per car, or $5 per person on foot, motorcycle or bicycle.

Backpackers will want to visit one of the park's two hiking centers before taking off, to register and find out about current trail conditions. There is one at **Longmire [19]**, on the road between the Nisqually entrance and Paradise, and another at the **White River [20]** entrance. The staff can guide you to a trail right for your skills and schedule.

There are 5 drive-up and more than 40 hike-in campgrounds within the park, plus dozens more in the surrounding area. Park campgrounds generally have plenty of space Sunday thru Thursday, but fill up real early on weekends.

Backcountry permits are necessary for all overnight hiking trips.

Paradise [21] has a 360 degree view, several hiking trails, an interpretive display, visitors center, snack bar, gift shop and a historic inn. The center is open on weekends year round, and weekdays from late April to early October. The road from the Nisqually Entrance to Paradise is paved, and generally open throughout the winter.

Sunrise [22] is another great place for hiking. Located at an elevation of 6,400 feet, it is closed from mid September to mid June. This is the highest point in the park accessible to automobiles, and offers a number of spectacular roadside views.

In all, Mt. Rainier National Park has 305 miles of maintained trails. Several excellent family hikes begin in the lower elevation campgrounds. Hikers should plan on leaving their dogs at home, as pets are not permitted in the park's backcountry areas or on its trails.

Wonderland Trail [23], at 93 miles, is the longest park trail. It takes about 10 days to hike, and circles the mountain, crossing alpine meadows, glacial streams, mountain passes and forested valleys. This steep loop trail is only for the hardy hiker; camps are about 10 miles apart.

Good short hikes include the **Nisqually River Trail [24]** out of Cougar Rock Campground, the loop trail over **Rampart Ridge [25]**, and scenic **Silver Falls Loop [26]**. The hike up **Gobbler's Knob [27]** is a little steeper, but will take you to one of the park's best viewpoints.

You will also find several easy, **self-guided nature trails [28]**.

Glaciers are one of the park's biggest attractions, but can also be the most dangerous. On warm days, avalanches of ice, snow and rock make being near glaciers dangerous. These come without sound or warning, and sometimes last five minutes. Mudflows too can come suddenly as the melting glaciers release huge quantities of water, mud and rock from beneath its mass, so be careful.

Wildlife is plentiful, and the observant visitor might see deer, elk, bear, beaver, mountain lion, raccoons or ptarmigan from a distance. If you intend to fish, check with the park rangers; some areas are closed to all fishing and others open only to fly-fishing.

For Additional Information

If you plan to visit Mount St. Helens or Rainier, you should call some of the following agencies. They can provide maps and other information.

Gifford Pinchot National Forest
(360) 891-5000

Mt. St. Helens NVM Headquarters
(360) 247-3900

Mt. St. Helens Visitors Center
(360) 274-2100

Randle Ranger District
(360) 497-1100

Packwood Ranger District
(360) 494-0600

Mt. Rainier National Park Hdqtrs.
(360) 569-2211

Mt. St. Helens/Rainier Area Accommodations

CASTLE ROCK

Blue Heron Inn B&B
(360) 274-9595 or (800) 959-4049
2846 Spirit Lake Hwy.
6 view rooms w/pri. bath & balcony,
no smoking, disabled access, jacuzzi
suite, $115-195, inc. full breakfast.

Mt. St. Helens Motel
(360) 274-7721
1340 Mt. St. Helens Way NE
32 rooms, pets okay, disabled access,
$42-70.

7 West Motel
(360) 274-7526
864 Walsh Rd. NE
24 rooms, pets okay, $35-51.

Silver Lake Motel & Resort
(360) 274-6141
3201 Spirit Lake Hwy. - Silver Lake
6 rooms plus 5 cabins - all w/kitchen
facilities, pets okay in cabins, on Silver
Lake, $55-75.

Timberland Inn
(360) 274-6002
1271 Mt. St. Helens Way
40 rooms w/refrigerators, jacuzzi suite
& non-smoking rooms, pets okay, disabled access, nearby rest., $45-120.

COUGAR

Lone Fir Resort
(360) 238-5210
16806 Lewis River Rd.
16 rooms & suites plus 4 bedroom
house, no smoking or pets, summer
pool & snack bar, near rest., $40-85.

Monfort's B&B
(360) 238-5229
132 Cougar Loop Rd.
2 rooms w/pri. bath, disabled access,
hot tub, no smoking, $65-76, inc. full
breakfast.

CRYSTAL MOUNTAIN

Alpine Inn
(360) 663-2262
One Crystal Mountain Blvd.
34 rooms, restaurant, $40-88.

Silver Skis Chalet Condos
(360) 663-2558
One Crystal Mountain Blvd.
60 condo units, no smoking, pool,
exercise room, $105-190.

Village Inn Hotel
(360) 663-2558
One Crystal Mountain Blvd.
20 rooms, no smoking, exercise room,
$62-85.

ELBE/ASHFORD AREA

Gateway Inn B&B
(360) 569-2506
State Hwy. 706 - Ashford
9 modern log cabins plus 18 RV sites
w/full hookups and grassy tent area,
walk to restaurant & store, cabins
$70/night - campground $9-15.

Hobo Inn
(360) 569-2500
54104 Mountain Hwy. E - Elbe
8 rooms, no smoking, pets okay, inc.
full breakfast, $70-85/night.

Jasmer's Guesthaus & Cabins
(360) 569-2682
30005 State Hwy. 706 - Ashford
8 rooms, private baths, hot tub, $45-
125, inc. cont. breakfast.

Mountain Meadows Inn B&B
(360) 569-2788
28912 State Hwy. 706E - Ashford
6 rooms, private baths, no smoking,
$75-110, inc. full breakfast.

Mounthaven Resort
(360) 569-2594
38210 State Hwy. 706E - Ashford
12 rooms, pets okay, $50-150.

Mt. Rainier Country Cabins
(360) 569-2355
Ashford
10 cabins, pets okay, no smoking,
nearby restaurant, $45-75.

Nisqually Lodge
(360) 569-8804
31609 State Hwy. 706 - Ashford
24 rooms, disabled access, no smoking, hot tub, restaurant, $50-97, inc.
cont. breakfast.

Rainier Overland
(360) 569-0851
31811 State Hwy. 706E - Ashford
12 rooms, disabled access, no smoking, $65-165.

Whittakers Bunkhouse
(360) 569-2439
30205 State Hwy. 706E - Ashford
19 rooms, many w/private bath, disabled access, no smoking, hot tub,
$20-80.

MORTON

Evergreen Motel
(360) 496-5407
Main St. at Front St.
12 rooms, pets okay, nearby restaurant, $30-50.

Seasons Motel
(360) 496-6835
200 Westlake Ave.
50 rooms, non-smoking & disabled
access rooms available, small pets
w/approval, $55-65.

St. Helens Manorhouse B&B
(800) 551-3290
4 rooms, dis. access, pets okay, no
smoking, hot tub, $65-95, inc. break.

MT. RAINIER NAT'L PARK

Longmire Inn
(360) 569-2400
Located east of Ashford - in park - at
2,700' elev.
25 rooms - many w/private baths, no
smoking, lounge w/fireplace, open
year round, restaurant, $66-91.

Paradise Inn
(360) 569-2275
Located northeast of Ashford - in Mt.
Rainier National Park - at 5,400' elev.
126 rooms - many w/private baths, no
smoking, disabled access, restaurant
& lounge, open mid May to October,
$69-98.

PACKWOOD

Cowlitz River Lodge
(888) 881-0379
32 rooms, hot tub, disabled access,
$50-60, inc. cont. breakfast

Hotel Packwood (360) 494-5431
104 Main St.
9 rooms, pets okay, $20-38.

Mountain View Lodge (360) 494-5555
13163 US Hwy. 12
24 rooms, pool, hot tub, pets okay,
$31-73.

Tatoosh Meadows Resort
(800) 294-2311 or (360) 494-2311
On Cowlitz River
11 cabins, pets okay, hot tub, located
on 32 acres, $100-300.

Tatoosh Motel (360) 494-5321
12880 US Hwy. 12
14 rooms, hot tub, $29-125, inc. cont.
breakfast.

RANDLE

Mt. Adams Motel
(360) 497-7007
661 Cispus Rd.
16 rooms, disabled access, pets okay,
ex. room, campground - tents & RV
sites, rooms $35-45.

Randle Motel
(360) 497-5346
9780 US Hwy. 12
10 rooms, $35-45.

Woodland Motel
(360) 494-6766
11890 US Hwy. 12
8 rooms, pets okay, $30-65.

Mt. St. Helens/Rainier Campgrounds & RV Parks

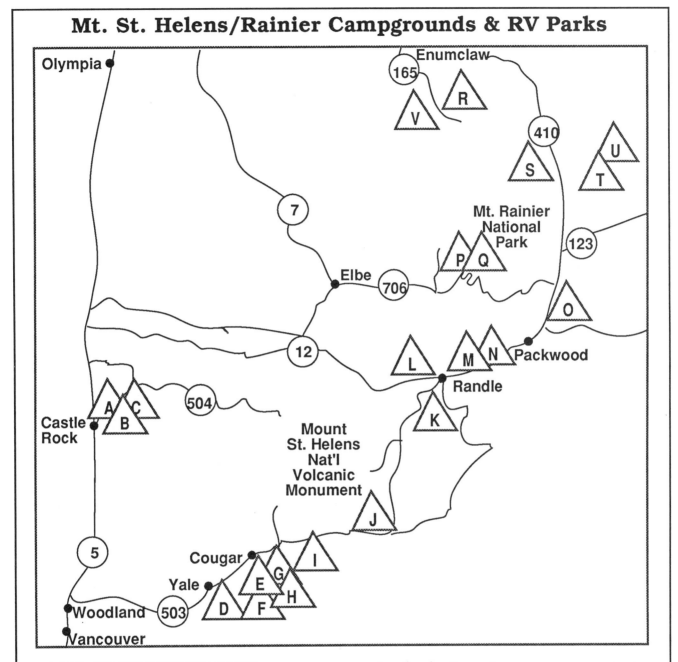

A) MT. ST. HELENS RV PARK

88 units - 49 w/full hookups, 30 w/water-elec.-cable plus tent sites, (360) 274-8522, trailers to 70', showers, disabled access, trailer waste disposal, pets okay, open year round, $15 to $20/night.

Take State Hwy. 504 east of Castle Rock 2 miles. Located on hill behind grocery store, at 167 Schaffan Rd.

B) SEAQUEST STATE PARK

16 campsites w/full hookups plus 76 standard sites, group area - reservations (360) 274-8633, trailers to 50', showers, disabled access, trailer waste disposal, fishing, $10 to $15/night - groups $25/night plus $1/person.

Follow State Hwy. 504 east of Castle Rock for about 5 miles and watch for signs.

C) CEDARS RV PARK

26 sites w/full hookups plus tent area, showers, laundry, pets okay, hiking trails, $11 to $15/night.

Leave I-5 at exit #46 and go to 115 Beauvais Rd.

C) FOX PARK RV

52 units - 44 w/full hookups, 8 w/water & elec., plus grassy tent area, some 60' pull thru sites, reservations (360) 274-6785, small pets okay, showers, laundry, near Toutle & Cowlitz Rivers, $12 to $15/night.

Leave I-5 at exit #52 (Toutle Park Rd.) and go to 112 Burma Rd.

D) CRESAP BAY CAMP

58 units plus large group area, reservations (503) 464-5035, showers, handicap access, trailer waste disposal, on Lake Merwin, boat ramp, moorage, swimming, fishing, water skiing, interpretive trail, open summer only, campsites $15/night - groups $225.

Take State Hwy. 503 east of Yale 2 miles and follow Lewis River Highway south 4 miles to camp.

E) COUGAR RV PARK

14 sites w/full hookups plus 7 tent sites, reservations (360) 238-5224, trailers to 70', showers, pets okay, open year round, $10 to $14/night.

Located at 16730 Lewis River Road, in Cougar.

F) LONE FIR RESORT

32 units w/hookups plus grassy tent area, reservations (360) 238-5210, trailers to 40', showers, laundry, ice, pool, pets okay, $13 to $18/night.

In Cougar, on Lewis River Road.

G) COUGAR CAMP

45 tent sites plus large group area, reservations (503) 464-5035, showers, handicap access, playground, on Yale Reservoir, boat launch, fishing, swimming, water skiing, open summer only, campsites $12/night - groups $225.

East of Cougar 1 mile on State Hwy. 503.

H) BEAVER BAY CAMP

63 units plus large group area, reservations (503) 464-5035, flush toilets, showers, handicap access, trailer waste disposal, playground, on Yale Reservoir, boat launch, fishing, swimming, water skiing, open May thru Oct., campsites $15/night - groups $225.

Go east of Cougar 2 miles on State Hwy. 503.

I) SWIFT CAMP

93 units, trailers okay, flush toilets, handicap access, trailer waste disposal, on Swift Reservoir, boat launch, fishing, swimming, water skiing, open May thru Oct., $15/night.

Take State Hwy. 503 east of Cougar 18 miles and FSR 90 to campground.

J) LOWER FALLS REC. AREA NATIONAL MONUMENT CAMP

43 units - includes 2 multi-family units & 1 group site, reservations (800) 280-CAMP, maximum site 60' - some paved, on Lewis River, vault toilets, waterfalls - accessible trail, pets okay, open mid May thru Labor Day, elev. 1300', $9/night - $18 for multi-family units and $22 and up for group site.

Take State Hwy. 503 east of Cougar 18 miles and FSR 90 north 12 miles - located at monument headquarters.

K) IRON CREEK FS CAMP

98 units - 81 single sites plus 17 multi-family sites, maximum 42', reservations (800) 280-CAMP, on Cispus River, fishing, hiking, old-growth trees, accessible trail along creek, open mid May thru mid Oct., elev. 1200', $10/night - multi-family sites $20.

Take State Hwy. 131 south of Randle 3 miles and FSR 25 southwest 9 miles.

L) COWLITZ FALLS COUNTY PARK

12 units w/water & elec., 73 w/out hookups plus group area, tents okay, reservations (360) 497-7175, trailers to 36', showers, wheelchair access, trailer waste disposal, on Lake Scanwa, boat ramp & dock, fishing, pets okay, open May thru Oct., $9 to $13/night - call for information on group area.

Take US Hwy. 12 west of Randle 2 miles and Peters Rd. south to park.

L) TOWER ROCK U-FISH RV

29 units w/hookups plus tent area, reservations (360) 497-7680, trailer waste disposal, fishing, $12-14/night.

Located in Randle, at 137 Cispus Rd.

M) PACKWOOD RV PARK

69 units w/hookups plus grassy tent area, pets okay, showers, trailer waste disposal, walk to stores & restaurants.

Located right in Packwood - behind the library (next to city park).

M) SHADY FIRS RV PARK & CAMP

40 units - 17 w/hookups + tent area, reservations (360) 497-6108, trailers to 70', showers, laundry, playground, horses & pets okay, fishing, swimming, trailer waste disposal, open year round, $8 to $14/night.

Take US Hwy. 12 east of Randle 3 miles - located at 107 Young Rd.

N) LA WIS WIS FS CAMP

105 units - a few RVs to 24', 20 multi-family sites plus walk-in tent sites, flush toilets, limited wheelchair access, picnic area, river, fishing, hiking, elev. 1400', $10 to $16/night.

Take US Hwy. 12 east of Packwood 7 miles to campground road.

O) OHANAPECOSH NP CAMP

232 units, trailers to 30', trailer waste disposal, hiking, old growth trees, on Ohanapecosh River, fishing, closes in late Oct., elev. 2000', $12/night.

Take US Hwy. 12 east of Packwood 8 miles and State Hwy. 123 north 4 miles. This campground is located 1.5 miles south of Mt. Rainier National Park entrance.

P) COUGAR ROCK NP CAMP

200 campsites plus group area, trailers to 30', for information on group area call (360) 569-2211, trailer waste disposal, hiking, closes in mid Oct., elev. 3100', $10/night.

Take State Hwy. 706 east of Elbe 22.2 miles. This campground is located .8 mile east of the Nisqually Entrance to Mt. Rainier National Park.

Q) SUNSHINE POINT NP CAMP

20 units, trailers to 25', on Nisqually River, fishing, elev. 2000', $10/night.

Take State Hwy. 706 east of Elbe 22.6 miles. This campground is located .5 mile east of the Nisqually Entrance to Mt. Rainier National Park.

R) IPSUT CREEK NP CAMP

32 units, trailers to 20', hiking, elev. 4400', $10/night.

Take State Hwy. 165 to Carbonado. This campground is located 5 miles east of Mt. Rainier National Park's Carbon River Entrance.

S) SILVER SPRINGS FS CAMP

56 units, trailers to 22', reservations (800) 280-2267, picnic area, wheelchair access, fishing, elev. 2600', $8 to $10/night.

Follow State Hwy. 410 southeast of Enumclaw 31.3 miles. This campground is located 1 mile north of the Mt. Rainier National Park boundary.

T) CORRAL PASS FS CAMP

20 tent units, stream, near Mountain Goat Reserve & Norse Peak Wilderness, berry picking, primitive, horse ramp, elev. 5600', $5/night.

Located southeast of Enumclaw. Take State Hwy. 410 southeast of town 31 miles and FSR 7174 east 6.1 miles.

U) ECHO LAKE FS CAMP

13 units, hike-in only, no drinking water, shelter, swimming, fishing, elev. 3800', no fee.

Take State Hwy. 410 southeast of Enumclaw 32.1 miles, FSR 185 east 6.7 miles, and hike Trail #1176 northeast 5.2 miles.

V) WHITE RIVER NP CAMP

112 campsites plus group camp, trailers to 20', on White River, hiking, $10/night.

Follow State Hwy. 410 southeast of Enumclaw 36 miles. This campground is located 5 miles west of the White River Entrance for Mt. Rainier National Park.

ABOUT THE AUTHOR

KiKi Canniff is a Pacific Northwest writer who specializes in books about Oregon & Washington. She is the Portland Oregonian's former campground columnist, and an avid outdoorswoman. KiKi also enjoys hiking, travel, history, nature, and exploring Pacific Northwest backroads.

ORDER COUPON

Please send the following books:

___ **Great Vacations in Oregon & Washington** @ $18.50 ea.   _____
___ **The Northwest Golfer – 4th Ed**. @ $14.95 ea.   _____
___ **Northwest Free: Historic Attractions** @ $10.95 ea.   _____
___ **A Camper's Guide to Oregon & Washington** @ $14.95 ea. _____
(*Free shipping w/order for 2 or more books)   Shipping __3.00*__
                                        Total Amount Enclosed _____

Name _____
Address _____
City/State/Zip Code_____

To order: Check with your local bookseller, or send this form with your check or money order to Ki² Enterprises, 1214 Wallace Road NW #165, Salem, Oregon 97304.

GV98

- -

Please send:
___ **Great Vacations in Oregon & Washington** @ $18.50 ea.   _____
___ **The Northwest Golfer – 4th Ed**. @ $14.95 ea.   _____
___ **Northwest Free: Historic Attractions** @ $10.95 ea.   _____
___ **A Camper's Guide to Oregon & Washington** @ $14.95 ea. _____
(*Free shipping w/order for 2 or more books)   Shipping __3.00*__
                                        Total Amount Enclosed _____

Name _____
Address _____
City/State/Zip Code _____

To order: Check with your local bookseller, or send this form with your check or money order to Ki² Enterprises, 1214 Wallace Road NW #165, Salem, Oregon 97304.

GV98

INDEX